How to Negotiate Like A

Like A

Pro

How to | Negotiate
Like A
Pro

How to Resolve Anything, Anytime, Anywhere

Third Edition

MARY GREENWOOD

HOW TO NEGOTIATE LIKE A PRO
HOW TO RESOLVE ANYTHING, ANYTIME, ANYWHERE

iUniverse books may be ordered through booksellers or by contacting:

iUniverse
1663 Liberty Drive
Bloomington, IN 47403
www.iuniverse.com
1-800-Authors (1-800-288-4677)

Because of the dynamic nature of the Internet, any web addresses or links contained in this book may have changed since publication and may no longer be valid. The views expressed in this work are solely those of the author and do not necessarily reflect the views of the publisher, and the publisher hereby disclaims any responsibility for them.

Any people depicted in stock imagery provided by Thinkstock are models, and such images are being used for illustrative purposes only.
Certain stock imagery © Thinkstock.

ISBN: 978-1-5320-3116-8 (sc)
ISBN: 978-1-5320-3117-5 (e)

Library of Congress Control Number: 2017912919

Print information available on the last page.

iUniverse rev. date: 09/08/2017

Contents

Preface

How to Negotiate Like a Pro, How to Resolve Anything, Anytime, Anywhere, Third Edition

How to Negotiate Like a Pro, winner of 9 book awards, was the first of my three "how to" books on negotiations. The second book was *How to Mediate Like a Pro, 42 Rules for Mediating Disputes,* winner of 12 book awards, and the third book was *How to Interview Like a Pro, 43 Rules for Getting Your Next Job*, winner of 12 book awards.

I have been negotiating most of my professional career as an attorney, mediator, human resources director, union negotiator, law school professor and Mother. As a union negotiator, I started noticing certain characteristics or rules in negotiations that were settled that were not present in the disputes that were not settled. I started jotting down a list of these characteristics or rules to assist me in negotiating future union agreements. As I reviewed my list, I realized that these rules did not apply just to union negotiations, but they also applied to any kind of dispute, including negotiations with a boss, a spouse, siblings, banks, credit card companies, hotels, restaurants, and buyers and sellers on eBay. That was my "aha moment" and I decided to write *How to Negotiate Like a Pro, 41 Rules for Resolving Disputes.*

In 2012, I updated and revised *How to Negotiate Like a Pro* with a second edition. In this new 2017 third edition, *How to Negotiate like a Pro, How to Resolve Anything, Anytime, Anywhere*, I have updated and reorganized the 41 rules, and added new chapters: **Chapter 5. How to Apologize Like a Pro; Chapter 7. How to Negotiate with Difficult People; and Chapter 15. A Summary of the 41 rules.**

I added a new chapter about negotiating with difficult people, like pathological liars, bullies and narcissists, because I have noticed that since the second edition was published, there is much more anger and resentment in negotiations, in the workplace as well as in society in general. People are much more willing to be argumentative just for the sake of stirring the pot.

The country seems much more divisive and people seem to be more willing to lie or call something fake news than they were five years ago. Everyone seems to be on edge. I have also added many new tips to help you negotiate no matter who is at the other end of the negotiating table.

After you read *How to Negotiate Like a Pro, How to Resolve Anything, Anytime, Anywhere*, Third Edition, you will be negotiating like a pro, especially when dealing with difficult people.

Acknowledgments

I would like to acknowledge my mom and dad, who taught me a sense of fairness, and my two sisters, Marnie and Sara, for forcing me to learn negotiating at an early age.

I want to thank my son, John, a Judge, an attorney, and mediator, who knew intuitively how to negotiate at age five, and his wife, Astrid, who can negotiate in French and English. My two grandsons, Jack and Gage, eleven and nine, keep me on my toes and help me keep my negotiation skills current.

I also want to thank Dr. Joseph Pizzolatto and Mount Sinai Cancer Center in Miami Beach who have helped me be cancer free for over 11 years.

I also want to thank my dear friends, Paula Felici and Nadine Salazar, for their support, suggestions and proofreading skills.

Introduction

The format of *How to Negotiate Like a Pro, How to Resolve Anything, Anytime, Anywhere,* Third Edition, is to list each of the 44 rules and explain what it means and how to use it in negotiations. At the end of each rule is a script so that the readers can use the actual language of the script in their negotiations if they choose. Not every rule or script will be used in each negotiation. The intent is to provide a variety of rules so that readers can pick and choose those that are helpful to their individual situations.

How to Negotiate Like a Pro, How to Resolve Anything, Anytime, Anywhere, Third Edition, will help you prepare and research for negotiations. It will help you deal with people who are unreasonable, unpredictable and complicated, including those are who narcissists, unethical and pathological liars. It will give you strategies and practical tips for the negotiation process. It will also give you some insight as to what the other side is thinking and help you break a deadlock. *How to Negotiate Like a Pro* will also give you specific tips for negotiating with your boss, your spouse, and service providers such as the phone company, car dealers, and hotels.

At the end of the book are appendices to give the reader some reference materials, including a Glossary of Negotiation Terms, About the Author page and and a list of Book Awards.

Chapter 1 | Preliminaries for Negotiations

Negotiation is a process whereby parties resolve disputes. The essence of the negotiation process is that the parties agree to work with each other to resolve a problem or a dispute. The word *negotiation* is sometimes used synonymously with *bargaining*. This can be a simple negotiation with your spouse as to who takes out the trash, or a complex negotiation that determines salary increases that affect thousands of employees.

The language used for negotiation is very colorful and diverse. Many of the terms and expressions are borrowed from other disciplines or endeavors such as poker (bargaining chip); war (smoke screen); tennis (the ball is in your court); duck hunting (decoy); fox hunting (red herring); politics (saving face and impasse); religion (devil's advocate), and labor /management (Boulewareism). The Glossary of Negotiation Terms found in Appendix A gives detailed definitions of terms used throughout the book. Many of these terms will also be explained in more detail as they are used throughout the book.

Before getting into the nitty-gritty of research and preparing draft resolutions, let's focus on some preliminaries to be in the right frame of mind for negotiations.

Rule 1. Focus on the goal. Don't be distracted by your emotions

It is important to check your emotions at the door before trying to negotiate anything. Emotions such as anger can make one lose control. We have all seen someone who gets red in the face and starts shaking his finger and generally looks as though he could easily have a heart attack. Sometimes that person is so mad that he is incoherent. You need to get past that stage if you are going to succeed. One way to prevent angry outbursts is to include them in your ground rules at the first negotiating session. (See Rule 11, *Request ground rules,* and Appendix C for sample policy.) Then it is understood that tantrums and outbursts will not be tolerated. The ground rules set the boundaries for behavior in the negotiation. If the other side has an outburst, nip it in the bud. If you allow tantrums in the beginning, it will set a bad precedent, and it will look as though you are condoning discourteous behavior.

If you are the one who is angry and upset, you need to focus on what you hope to accomplish and tell yourself that nothing is going to stand in the way of that goal. If you feel yourself getting upset during negotiations, ask for a break and try to regain your composure. Before you return to the room, take a deep breath in through the nose and all the way to the stomach and then breathe out two or three times. This can help you relax and help you concentrate on keeping your emotions in check.

It really does not matter whether or not you like the other side. Some parties are rude, obnoxious, and insulting. For example, in a divorce proceeding, just seeing the other side can make the parties angry. This does not mean that it is impossible to resolve your dispute, although it may be more difficult. Try to get past these insults so you can focus on resolving the dispute. The other side may be baiting you, so don't give it the satisfaction of knowing it has gotten to you. If you focus on the goals of the negotiation, it won't matter whether you like or respect the other party.

If you know that you cannot work with the other party, you have to make a decision as to whether to proceed with the negotiation. If you find that you cannot focus on your goals because you cannot control your feelings, you may want to consider a different forum, such as mediation or arbitration. Or you may want to hire an attorney to represent you. Then you won't have to deal directly with the other person. If you do proceed, don't let your emotions interfere with the negotiation.

Script:

I know we have had problems in the past, but I believe that if we are courteous to each other and abide by our ground rules, we can come to an agreement.

I appreciate that negotiations can get emotional, but I am asking you to control your outbursts. Unless they stop, I will request a break or stop the session for today.

I am going to pretend I did not hear that comment and move right along, but consider this a warning that such comments will not be tolerated in the future.

Rule 2. Look forward, not back. The past is called the past for a reason.

One party may revel in detailing everything (and I mean everything,) that has happened in the dispute so far and insist on documenting each episode or incident from the very beginning even if these took place several years ago. If one party gets too involved in what has happened in the past, it can be counterproductive. The husband in a divorce case may be so intent on documenting everything the wife has done wrong that the husband is not even thinking about the goals of the negotiation beyond blaming the wife.

Looking back at the past usually doesn't help current negotiations. You have to figure out a way to get to the present and deal with current issues that need to be resolved like custody or visitation. Ask the other party what they want now to resolve the dispute. This usually brings the parties to the present, especially if they have not considered what exactly it is they want. Another way is to let the other side vent about the grievances of the past to clear the air, preferably in a caucus setting, (see Glossary) where the other side can't hear. Make clear that the intent of a settlement is not to punish either party but a way to resolve the dispute. If the other side cannot let go of the emotional wounds of the past, the parties may not be able to agree to a settlement. You may want to reconsider whether negotiation is the appropriate forum. You may want to consider whether mediation with a third-party facilitator is the proper place to resolve the dispute. Mediation often works well in divorce disputes.

Script:

This is probably my fault. Let's look to the future not the past.

What exactly do you want to resolve this dispute?

Rule 3. You don't have to be right to settle.

What are the three words we want to hear the most, even more than "I Love you?" We love to hear those magic words, "You are right." For some people, this is even harder to say than "I love you." And if you say, "You are absolutely right," that is even better. When someone says, "It is the principle that counts" or "It is not the money; it's the principle," I know that the negotiation is in trouble. That is because the party is making a judgment call that it is more important to be a martyr than to settle the case. When someone is obsessed with the principle of a situation, she is still emotionally vested in her feelings. Unless the parties can get beyond those emotions, the dispute is not likely to be resolved.

If the person with whom you are negotiating thinks he is always right, you can use this to your advantage. Since the other side has told you, "it is not the money but the principle," you may be able to give an apology, change your procedures, or do something else that allows the other side to stay within its principles and feel vindicated. Find something to agree with no matter how small. You have to get beyond who is right and who is wrong and get to what is going to resolve the case. Feeling that you are right can be a heady emotion, but it has no place in the negotiation process.

To use one of my Mother's favorite phrases, "flattery gets you everywhere." First of all, don't be argumentative or criticize an incorrect statement. That just escalates the discussion getting nowhere fast. Try a little flattery. Try saying, "you are absolutely right" and see if the mood changes.

It is not always someone's fault. There are situations when no one is to blame, and there is no right or wrong side. Both sides assume the other person has done something wrong and is lying and untrustworthy. Try to get beyond the immediate distrust and ask factual questions about the problem. Sometimes an innocent mistake has been made by one of the parties, who did not even realize it. Sometimes the mistake was made by a third party. Parties who are concerned with who is at fault rather than how to settle often don't want to compromise. If you want the negotiation to move forward, you may have to be the first to start the initiative and even accept some of the blame. An apology can go a long way to resolve a dispute. If the other side is only interested in being right, chances are the situation won't be resolved. As my Mother also used to say, "You can lead a horse to water, but you can't make him drink." Give it your best shot and then you may have to accept that this dispute won't be resolved.

Script:

I know that you think this is my fault, and maybe it is. How can we get beyond this blame game and move forward to a solution?

You know, you are absolutely right. I made a big mistake. I want to apologize and hope you can forgive me. How would you like to proceed?

I don't think this was anyone's fault. I believe it was an honest mistake. Let's try to get to the bottom of this.

Chapter 2 | How to Prepare for Negotiations

Rule 4. Know what you want and what the other side wants.

Preparation can be the most important phase of negotiations. There is no such thing as being over-prepared. Knowing what you want may seem obvious, but many parties don't know what they want. They are so angry that they have not even asked themselves how the issue can be resolved. If they don't know what they want, how can they go about getting it? Instead, they may want to hash and rehash the circumstances that got them into this negotiation.

Depending on the complexity of the situation, you should have a detailed plan of what you want. Even more importantly, you also need to know what you are willing to give up in order to get what you want. Generally you can get what you want if you give the other party something it wants. My motto is "eveything is negotiable." Don't ever begin a negotiation without knowing what you want.

Knowing what the other side wants is a little more difficult than knowing what you want. You cannot be certain if your assessment is accurate. How do you find out? Sometimes just asking the other side what it wants will give you some idea of its goals. However, you may need to take the response with a grain of salt. You can also look at previous negotiations if you have the records. In union negotiations, parties often ask for the same thing year after year. Sometimes the only way you can know is by making a counteroffer to something they offered you. An eager acceptance of a counteroffer can give you some insight.

In your first offer, you need to ask for more than you actually want so you can leave room for compromise and bargaining. This can be tricky. If you ask for too much, you might not be taken seriously. If you ask for too little, you might be leaving money on the table.

Although it is unlikely a party will tell you outright all they want, looking at body language can help. An expression such as a sneer or a smirk might give something away. If a party is suddenly very interested in what you're saying, this might be a "hot topic." On the other hand, disinterest may be real or feigned. If you hear murmurs or mumblings by the team, you can get an idea whether you have hit a "hot topic."

You can also ask the other side to prioritize its issues. Sometimes the other side wants something that is not important to you. If you can find out what that something is, perhaps you can trade something for it. You may have a hunch about what the other side wants, but be sure to follow it up with facts and research.

Script:

Can you tell me why you want this provision?

Can you make a counteroffer?

Can you prioritize these three issues so we know where to start?

I have prepared a proposal and would like a response from you.

Rule 5. Be prepared, and do your research.

Once you have an idea what you want, you must do your research and preparation to solidify your position. That could be as simple as listing your arguments on a sheet of paper or as complex as doing the research to cost out a request for wage increases. Either way, you need to be prepared. Otherwise, you might make a concession (see glossary, Appendix A) or agreement that you will later regret. You need to know the rationale behind your requests and have a good estimate of the costs, including the future costs. If the negotiation is a complex one, you may want to consider an expert to do the number crunching for you.

What do you do if the other side does not believe research is that important? Some negotiators use a big picture approach and do not have a fine eye for detailed provisions. Even if the other side has not done its research, that is even more reason for you to do yours.

In a negotiation such as a union negotiation, much preliminary work needs to be done. When doing a proposal for wage increases, for example, internal information must be collected, such as the number of employees, salaries, and pay grades, as well as information from departments in other cities in the county and neighboring counties that are comparable. When you collect statistics, you need to see if they are prepared the same way you are preparing your comparable numbers. It is very important that your statistics are accurate and in a format that is easily understood and explained.

Nothing is more embarrassing than making a presentation and having someone question the accuracy of your numbers and having the whole presentation fall apart because the data is confusing or, even worse, incorrect. Sometimes the other side will have its own set of data. If you can get the other side to agree with your data, it will make the negotiation run more smoothly. Even if the other side does not agree with your numbers, it will still be helpful if the other side can agree on the methodology or format. It may take more effort on your part, but it is always an advantage to work from your statistics or your drafts, especially if the other side approves them.

If you are not completely prepared, consider delaying the start of the negotiation. If you try to wing it, you will regret it later. You cannot be over-prepared. Even if you don't use everything you prepared, it does not matter. It is important to have as much information and research as possible just in case you need it. Of course, when something unforeseen comes up at the negotiating table, you can ask for time to research, but that can break the rhythm. The more you do in advance, the easier the negotiation will be. You should also expect the other side to be prepared. When it makes a proposal, you need to question how it arrived at its numbers.

Script:

Here is my first proposal, and I want to tell you how much this will cost in future years.

I am a little confused how you arrived at your numbers. I would like to know the process and rationale you used.

We are having our finance department work up some numbers. If both parties can agree on the methodology, then it will be a lot easier to negotiate pay increases.

Rule 6. Get a reality check. What is it really worth?

If a dispute is to be resolved, the parties have to be practical. When the party asks for something outrageous or unreasonable, there has to be a reality check. If you have done adequate preparation and research, you should be able to question a request that is not rational. Some parties start with totally exaggerated proposals just so they can give up something later on. Some parties have an inflated idea of the value of their items and think that (1) that they should make a large profit because they have kept something a long time; (2) that they should get the same price as a retail store; and (3) that their time and effort should be reflected in the price of an item.

Whether it is a car, a house, a pedigreed dog, or a collectible on eBay, you need to know what it is worth before you start the negotiation. You also need to set a spending or buying limit before you begin. If you are buying or selling something, you need to do some comparative shopping. A good source is the internet, especially eBay. Looking at selling prices for comparable items can be a good reality check. If you are checking comparable prices on eBay, look for the final sale amount, not the opening bid because the item might not actually be sold. An item is often worth a lot less than what you paid for it and less than a catalogue listing unless the item is extremely rare.

Be sure you are comparing apples to apples not apples to oranges. For example the value of a coin can be affected by the date, condition, and mintage. It is important to know the item's rarity. If something is readily available, a buyer might not offer much because she knows she can get it somewhere else. This is supply and demand. However, if an item is very rare, then the whole psychology is different. Now the buyer knows that if she does not buy it from you, she probably won't have another chance anytime soon to buy from anyone else, either.

Script:

The price of this item on eBay is 40 percent less than the catalogue.

This is very rare, and I doubt that another one will be available for a very long time.

Actually, $500 is a fair price since one just like it sold for $600 on eBay.

You only paid $25, and now you want $250 for your time and aggravation. My time is valuable, too, but I am not going to charge you for that.

Rule 7. Always have a Plan B.

It is an important strategy to have a backup plan or multiple backup plans. As they say, you should not put all your eggs in one basket. This means you have to be flexible. If one strategy does not work or is rejected, you need to move on and try something else. Some negotiators are not interested in any plan other than Plan A. They have a "take it or leave it" approach so that Plan B is not an option for them. This approach applies to labeling and perception. You may be able to get a provision depending on how it is labeled.

You can prepare your Plans B, C, and D by asking yourself questions that start with *how* or *what if*. How can I sweeten the deal? How can I close the deal? What if the party likes this? What if they reject this? The answers to these questions will help you come up with alternatives that will help close the deal. These alternatives can be bargaining chips (see glossary, Appendix A) when the need arises. If the other side is adamant about Plan A, perhaps you can incorporate some aspects of Plan B into Plan A.

Having a Plan B gets easier the more you negotiate. It becomes a way to be flexible and react to what the other side wants and to be able to think fast on your feet. If the only issue is price, then you can try to be flexible and come up with a group discount or a package deal for multiples items. If the other side won't budge on Plan A and you can't get it to accept any revisions, the negotiation may be doomed.

Script:

If you don't like that, I can show you something else.

I can give you a package deal. If you take this one, I will throw this one in for free.

If this does not work for you, let's go to Plan B.

Rule 8. Find out if the other side wants something other than money.

Sometimes the other party wants something other than money, such as time off or an apology. (see Rule 30). We are so used to negotiating about money that sometimes we forget that money is not everything. For example, a truly heartfelt apology can go a long way to resolving a consumer dispute. If the other side feels that the apology is sincere, the apology may even be enough to close the deal.

An employee might want time off instead of money. You may be able to suggest part-time work, flextime, or vacation time if the employee is one that you want to keep. These suggestions may be a way to resolve the problem and to save money at the same time. In a sexual harassment case, sometimes the complainant wants a change in policy, an acknowledgment that current policies are inadequate or a commitment to more workplace training.

Sometimes employees are more interested in convenience than money. For example, flexible time schedules are very popular. Some employees like to come in early and some employees like to leave early because of their children's school. Such policies don't cost money except for the administrative costs, but can build employee morale. Sometimes the other side wants something that is not important to you. If you can find out what that something is, it is a painless way of resolving a dispute. For example, an employee might want a raise and a new title. If you don't really care about the title change but don't have money for a raise at this time, perhaps you can offer the title change if the employee is willing to wait six months for the pay increase At least she gets something that she wants and knows she will be getting a raise soon. If you can keep what is important but make a concession on something else that is less important to you, that is good negotiations. Such alternatives are a win-win since they resolve the problem and save money at the same time.

If the non monetary alternatives don't solve the problem, then you may need to go back to your treasury and see if you can find some money to resolve the problem.

Script:

If we work together on the flexible time policy and it makes employees more productive, we would be more likely to approve it.

What is your first priority? We have limited resources, but if it is important to you, we might be able to work something out.

I can make that new title effective today if you wait six months for the raise.

Chapter 3 | NEGOTIATION STRATEGIES

Now that you have done your preparations and research, review the strategies that you can use in negotiations.

Rule 9. Only negotiate with someone with authority.

You need to determine whether you are negotiating with someone who has authority at the very beginning of the negotiations. Someone with authority (see glossary, Appendix A) is someone who can speak or act on behalf of the company or employer. If you are not dealing with someone with authority, then you are not really negotiating and are wasting everyone's time. This is important because you do not want to find out at the very end that the person with whom you thought you were negotiating did not have the authority to do so.

If you are not sure whether a person has authority to give you what you want, ask him directly. If you are in a more complex setting, you may ask for a written statement from the principal that this agent speaks or acts on his behalf. Sometimes someone will have the authority to act on someone else's behalf, but he may have restrictions such as a set monetary amount. For example, insurance agents may have the authority to settle a claim up to a certain amount. If that maximum amount is reached, then he would have to call his boss to see if he can get more authority. If the negotiator does not have authority, stop the negotiations until the negotiator gets that authority. If he cannot get authority, then stop the negotiations altogether.

Script:

Before we begin, I want to make sure that you have the authority to negotiate on this.

If you don't have authority, then we must stop negotiating.

Rule 10. Set the tone and look the part.

As in anything else in life, first impressions are very important. You don't get a second chance to make a first impression. You should set the tone of the negotiation when you come into the room for the first time. You should look and act like a professional. Project the image that you want to project and get to business quickly. Have a notebook and a briefcase and start right in. A nice handshake, not a bone breaker, and a warm smile continue the good impression.

If this is your first negotiation, you may want to practice in the mirror a few times. Practice what you are going to say so that you have a short speech prepared. You want the other side to know you are knowledgeable and have prepared for your first session. You don't want to hem and haw at the first negotiating session. Good eye contact is essential. Nothing makes a bad impression like not looking the other side in the eye and a half-hearted handshake.

I like to start by introducing myself; then I state what my philosophy of negotiations is and how I like to conduct my negotiations. I think of the qualities of a negotiator that I admire most and try to project them. For example, my idea of a good negotiator is someone who is firm, flexible, fair, honest, and has a good sense of humor. That is the tone I would like to set.

Script:

My approach to negotiation is based on trust.

I consider myself flexible, fair, and honest.

Just because I am negotiating does not mean I don't have a sense of humor.

Rule 11. Request ground rules.

At the first session, I usually ask the parties to agree to ground rules. A negotiation goes more smoothly if ground rules are adopted. Then if something goes awry, one can point out the ground rule that has been violated. (see Appendix C for a Sample Ground Rules Policy.)

The ground rules should set out the time and place for the negotiations. Rules concerning the procedures for each day are very important and will save you time in the long run. You can set out a timetable for the parties to follow. For example, the agenda will be prepared at the previous meeting, the proposals will be distributed at the second meeting, or the topics to be negotiated will be selected at the fourth meeting.

The role of the spokesperson needs to be spelled out. Is the spokesperson the only one allowed to accept and reject proposals or to request a caucus? Rules of conduct need to be addressed. Only one person will speak at any time and will not be interrupted. Everyone will speak with courtesy, and no profanity will be allowed. Both parties need to agree to comply with reasonable requests for information and pay reasonable reproduction costs. Special rules can be established on the use of cell phones, including where and when they are prohibited, and when they are allowed.

If you are negotiating with someone who does not want ground rules, the negotiation will generally take more time than with ground rules. The other side may like to be unpredictable and like to shake things up a bit. If the other side balks at ground rules, then there is not much you can do to enforce any. First I would give a little talk about how having ground rules sets out rules of courtesy and sets out the process so both sides know what they can or cannot do. If the other party still has no interest, I would see if it would agree to any of the ground rules. For example, having an agenda is important and not very controversial. It helps if both parties agree as to whether the spokesperson is the only one allowed to speak, accept and reject proposals or to request a caucus. The other side might agree to a rule concerning the spokesperson since the spokesperson is probably the chief negotiator, too. Ground rules concerning conduct and courtesy may be harder to enforce so I wouldn't spend a lot of time trying to get the other side to agree.

If I was negotiating without ground rules, I would politely stop the negotiations and give my objection to any swearing or objectionable behavior. Often the offending person is speaking out of turn, swearing or speaking over other team members so it is hard to take notes and to understand what is being said. I would ask the chief spokesperson, if the other side has one, to control its team member. I have not had a situation where ground rules were not accepted, but with a changing workplace, it could happen.

If you are negotiating with a team, internal rules need to be followed. If a team member wants to speak, he writes a note to the spokesperson to call a caucus. Negotiation materials must be kept secure. Don't leave them around during breaks or when you all leave the room. The negotiations are confidential and are not to be discussed outside the team. I like to give each team member an assignment. One can handle department issues; one can be the scribe and do all the paperwork; one can watch the other team to see how they react to proposals. It is important that all team members attend all sessions, except for an emergency, of course. The negotiations lose their flow if previous agreements have to be summarized again because a member was not present. It is also demoralizing to the team members who make the effort to attend all meetings. Letting the team members know in advance how important this is should reduce absenteeism.

Using the ground rules on the first session really helps set the tone for the negotiation. Everyone knows what is expected, and the negotiations become more professional. If both parties don't agree to ground rules, you can still have a good negotiation, but it may take longer.

Script:

Let's see if we can agree to a set of ground rules. If you like, I can draft a policy.

Ground rules set our expectations on how the negotiations will be conducted.

With ground rules, we can agree on a cell phone policy and common courtesy.

Rule 12. Volunteer and take control.

You want to get as much control of the negotiation as you can. One way you can do this is to volunteer anytime you can during the negotiation. Volunteer to:

A. Prepare the agenda.
B. Draft ground rules (see Rule 11) above.
C. Type up the minutes.
D. Get comparable statistics from the internet.
E. Prioritize and frame the issues.
F. Start first or give the first opening statement.
G. Anything else that gives you control of the paperwork.

Preparing the agenda is a tactical advantage because you can determine who goes first and make some preliminary suggestions as to the order and priority of negotiation topics. Being in charge of the note taking is also an advantage as long as it is done accurately and in a timely fashion. First of all it helps keep you organized by having someone take notes and make drafts. Using your computer and your software makes it less likely that a mistake is made as to the final language in the finished product.

If the other side is strapped for time or does not want to take on the responsibility of these projects, your offer may be accepted. Although volunteering may mean extra work, it will usually pay off in the long run. Volunteering is a way for you to control the negotiation and to get your opinions and solutions out front. Of course, if you are volunteering for a project such as doing the agenda or preparing notes, be sure that you spend enough time on this, and don't make mistakes. If you do sloppy work, then volunteering is not going to be an advantage. It could be a real detriment if you start confusing yourself and the other side.

Script:

I am willing to type up the day's notes and circulate them.

If you want, I can prepare the agenda for each meeting.

We can submit our proposals first if you like.

Rule 13. Agree on the issues and prioritize them.

If you volunteer to prioritize the issues, this saves a lot of time and effort. There may be areas that don't need amending and there is no need to even discuss them. Usually there are a few crucial issues that need to be negotiated. Some issues may be icing on the cake but not that important in the long run. Some negotiators want to negotiate every paragraph. Recognize this tactic for what it is, a strategy to prolong the negotiation process.

Prioritizing the issues can be tricky. You may not always want to go first. You may not want to divulge your priorities to the other side right away. If you can get the other side to tell you their priorities, this will help your own strategy. You can probably guess what the other side's priorities are, but you may be surprised. Prioritizing the issues helps move the negotiations forward.

Once you know what your issues are and their relative priority, you need to decide which ones to negotiate first. There are two schools of thought. Some negotiators like to start with the easy issues to gain some momentum and then move on to the more complicated items. Other negotiators like to start with a complex issue. When the difficult issues get resolved, the less important issues fall into place to complete the negotiation.

If you are negotiating with someone with a short attention span or this is your first negotiation, it is better to start with the easy items and work up to the more complicated ones. Resolving the smaller issues helps set the tone for the rest of the sessions. It develops mutual trust and respect that can carry on through the rest of the negotiation and it helps set the tone for the rest of the sessions. You can get bogged down very early in the negotiation if you begin with a complex issue like health care that can't easily get resolved.

Script:

Once we can prioritize the issues, we can develop a schedule.

Let's see if we can agree on some of the smaller issues before we move on to the more complex issues.

Let's start with the most difficult issue. Once that is resolved, it will be smooth sailing to resolve the other issues.

Rule 14. Say what you want.

This is a little different from knowing what you want. Even if you know what you want, you still have to articulate it properly. You need to determine how you are going to present what you want and the rationale behind it. In your first request, you generally need to ask for more than what you want so you can leave room for some bargaining and compromise. This can be tricky. If you ask for too much, you might not be taken seriously. If you don't ask for enough, you may end up compromising and getting less than you anticipated. Don't hem and haw and be indecisive. Be clear as to what your position is. If you have done your research and you have your Plan B, C, and D, you should have no problem with this rule.

Script:

I have one major goal in this negotiation, and this is it.

This is our first proposal, and this is why we think it is important.

Rule 15. Never take or give no for an answer.

If you ask for something you really want, and it is denied, don't take no for an answer. As they say, there is more than one way to skin a cat. Try to find out why the other side is saying no. Try to think of a different way to convince the other side to give you what you want. Go back to the drawing board and try to ask for what you want in a different way. Even a minor change, a compromise, or rephrasing might make it more palatable. If this is an important issue, suggest a trade-off or package deal, so the other side might be motivated by getting something it wants.

If you really want to resolve something, giving no as an answer does not help the negotiation. However, if you must say no, temper its effect so that it seems that you are willing to compromise or give some hope of a concession. Try to offer a scaled-down version of the original request if you have some leeway. If you absolutely must say no to the proposal, explain why you cannot go forward on this issue and counter with positive discussion on other issues. If you know this is an important issue for the other side, listen to its arguments very carefully so you can determine if its arguments would allow you to change your mind. Don't give up. You may be able to get something you really want in exchange.

Script:

We cannot agree to A, but I see some promise in B. Why don't you tell me what you are trying to accomplish in B, and maybe we can work something out.

I understand what you are saying, but what if we did it this way?

I am not sure why you are so opposed to this. Can you explain it to me?

Rule 16. It does not hurt to ask. If you don't ask, you don't get.

What if you want something you know the other side will not want to give you? How do you proceed? It does not hurt to ask; the worst that can happen is that the other person says no. This is true in any kind of negotiation, especially in dealing with your boss. Ask for that raise or promotion but give a rehearsed and researched speech on why you deserve it. Plan the timing of your request, too. If your boss says you did a good job on a recent project or you got an award from your peers, this would be a good time to give your rehearsed speech to remind your boss how valuable you are to the organization.

Even if you don't get it on the first request, your boss now knows what your goals are and may keep you in mind for future promotions. If you have a goal, let your boss know about it. Do your research and be prepared to defend what it is you want and why you should get it. If your boss denies your request, take it with grace, but ask questions as to what you can do in the future to prepare you for the next step. You might suggest a training class, working in another area to get more experience or working on a degree in your field. Don't think that if you deserve a raise or promotion, you will get it without initiating the conversation.

You can also use this rule if you have a bad customer service experience at a hotel or restaurant. Ask for something like an upgrade or a free night's stay if you are inconvenienced. You may be surprised and get it. If you don't ask, you don't get. So start asking.

Script:

Since you told me what a great job I did on that project, this may be a good time to discuss a promotion.

I have done a lot of research, and I am the lowest-paid department head in the city even though I have the most longevity.

I would like you to review my research and consider bringing my salary up to $80,000, which is the median salary for department heads.

I would like to go to the annual conference this year. It has many topics pertinent to that assignment you just gave me.

Rule 17. Don't give away bargaining chips without getting something in return.

This is a simple rule that is often violated. Sometimes it is tempting, especially at the beginning of the negotiation, to offer something to the other side to show how magnanimous you are. However, you are really giving away something for nothing, and that sets a bad precedent. You have your bargaining chips (see glossary), and you should get something for each one. Of course, if you can get something without even giving up something, that is even better.

Bargaining chips are something that can be offered to the other side in order to get a concession. It is important not to use all your chips in the beginning of the negotiation. It can be tempting to be generous when you first get started to create some momentum. However, you need to have some bargaining chips in reserve to help finalize the negotiations. You always want to end the negotiation with a few extra chips in reserve, not the other way around. The expression *bargaining chip* comes from the poker table, and you need to negotiate like a poker player with a poker face so the other side does not know what is "left in your cards."

Script:

I cannot give you something unless you give me something back.

I really don't have much else to give. I am tapped out. However, if we can finalize the negotiations today, I might be able to find some money for that project.

Rule 18. Always ask for one more thing or be prepared to give one more thing.

There are some people in a negotiation who are never going to be satisfied. Just when you think you have an agreement, they want one more thing. This is human nature, I guess, to squeeze as much out of the other side as possible. Knowing this trait will allow you to always keep a bargaining chip or two up your sleeve for when you are trying to wrap up negotiations. When the other side wants one last thing, then you can usually get one last thing as well.

The flip side is the same. If you are in a negotiation that is almost completed, the excitement rises as the last few issues are getting resolved. Always have a last-minute request to get another item into the agreement. Don't overuse this strategy because you may alienate the other side and find that you don't have any agreement at all.

A party is more likely to agree to these last-minute requests if it thinks it will finally resolve the dispute. However, it can backfire if the other side is offended that something new is being brought up at such a late time. Use judiciously. Remember there are some people who always have to have the last word. Use this trait to your advantage. Always have a bargaining chip up your sleeve.

Script:

If you can agree to this one last thing, I think we have an agreement.

If you give me my last request, I can agree to your last request, and we have a deal.

I thought we already had an agreement, and I am offended that you come back today asking for something else. You have gone too far!

Rule 19. Know the rhythm and tempo of the negotiation.

The tempo of a dispute resolution is very important. Even knowing someone's personality can be helpful. You need to read the other party and know how to deal with him. If you know the preferred tempo of the other side, you can use that to help resolve the case. Some parties want to go over every little detail and don't care if the session lasts all day or night. Others want to only look at the big picture and want to spend as little time on the details as possible. This knowledge can work to your advantage, especially when the tempo picks up at the end.

Sometimes, you may be surprised that the other side agreed to something you wanted. If this happens, consider yourself fortunate and move on to the next item. Don't overanalyze the agreement; act as though you were expecting it. The worst thing you can do is question it and say something like, "Are you sure you agree with the whole section?" Keep the momentum going, and consider yourself lucky.

The negotiation takes on a rhythm of its own, and you should respect that. Don't rush it, but don't let it get too long. Sometimes there are reasons that the other side does not want the negotiation to end. For example, employees might not want to go back to their regular jobs and hope to string out the negotiation sessions as long as possible since negotiations are a free pass from work. You need to be aware of the tempo, and adjust it when necessary. You will need to pick up the tempo if you are dealing with someone who can't make decisions and loves details. If you have agreed on some major provisions, you may want to suggest that the pace be picked up.

Script:

Now that we have agreed on some major provisions, I think we can pick up the pace.

We have really made some progress. However, I think we may be going a little too fast.

I would like to sleep on it and come back refreshed tomorrow.

Rule 20. Keep track of the paperwork.

You should volunteer to keep track of the paperwork. It means more work for you, but in the long run it will make the negotiations more efficient. By volunteering (see Rule 12 Volunteer and Take Control), you are in charge of keeping the paperwork straight. If you let the other side do it, you will still have to check the other side's work and make sure that the revisions are correct.

In a complex negotiation, it is very important to keep track of what has been approved and the history of all the revisions. One way to handle this is to have one person on your team be responsible to take notes and circulate the minutes at each meeting for approval. Be sure this person is detail-oriented and very computer literate. It is very important to number the drafts and put a date on each one so you know which version has been approved. That is why it is a good idea not to negotiate alone. It is very difficult to take notes when you are talking and reacting to what is being said all at the same time. The negotiator should always bring someone with her who is responsible for the minutes.

If you start getting confused as to the various drafts, mistakes will be made, and it will be a sign of weakness. Having the correct information is always a sign of strength. If you can provide the correct date, time, and content of previous discussions when there is a disagreement, you will be in control and have the advantage.

Script:

I went back into my notes and found we already approved that section on April 10.

We did not agree on that section yet. My notes say that we postponed that decision until we could get more information as to the cost.

Rule 21. Don't gloat.

If the negotiations seem to be going your way, and you are getting what you want, don't gloat or smirk. This might infuriate the other side. You should have a poker face so no one can tell how you think the negotiations are going. You may have to work on this because it is human nature to show a little emotion when things are going well. If the other side thinks you are gloating, it will know that you are happy about something that it gave away. It will really be on its guard, and the negotiations may even turn the other way. If you gloat, the other side will want to get something for its side so it can gloat, too.

However, if the other side likes to brag and gloat, you will have to ignore it. Let the other side gloat and don't let it bother you. You can even encourage it. Let the other side savor its win. The gloating negotiator may have a big ego and likes to think he is having lots of wins and successes. When he gloats, just let him take that moment. You can say something like, "That was a really good move. You should be proud of yourself."

Script:

Congratulations on a good negotiations. You did really well today.

I was just laughing at a joke someone told me this morning.

Rule 22. Be alert and keep a Poker Face

Be aware, and do not let your guard down. Even if you think the negotiations are going well, don't be lulled into complacency. Be vigilant and make sure you understand the ramifications of any provision. If you keep your poker face, it will be hard for the other side to interpret your moves. However, if your face shows your annoyance or frustration, the other side can use that information to its advantage.

Be careful what you say and how you say it. Everything you say should be planned and be part of your overall strategy. How you say it is also very important. Don't go off script unless you know the digression will benefit you. Keep watching the other side to see how it is reacting to the dynamics of the negotiation. Usually it is best to have a neutral demeanor and, occasionally, use some emotion to show what is really important to you. It is all in the delivery. Using the poker metaphor, keep your cards close to the vest so the other side will not know what's in your hand.

Script:

Don't let this demeanor fool you. I am paying attention.

I don't like to show my hand, but this item is very important to me.

Rule 23. Don't negotiate against yourself.

When you negotiate against yourself, you are making another offer when there is already an offer on the table. For example, if you make an offer of $10,000, and the other side does not answer or give a counteroffer, and then you offer $15,000, you are bidding or negotiating against yourself. Some inexperienced or impatient negotiators don't like silence. When you make an offer, you must be patient and wait for the other side to respond. Silence does not necessarily mean rejection, so resist that temptation to jump in with another offer.

It may be that the seller was willing to sell for $11,000, and you just lost $4,000 by not waiting for a counteroffer. When you are in a hurry, it is easy to leave money on the table. You get some indication that your offer is not high enough, and you start escalating the offers. However, it is always better to ask for a counteroffer. Make the other side do some work. If you are negotiating against yourself, you may actually pay more than what the other side was willing to accept. Tell the other side that you cannot make another offer until it makes you a counter-offer.

Script:

I feel as though I am negotiating against myself.

I cannot make you another offer until you make a counteroffer.

Rule 24. Be a devil's advocate.

The Roman Catholic Church used the devil's advocate to investigate candidates for sainthood to see if there was anything negative concerning their candidacy. The idea behind the devil's advocate is that if it is someone's job to do an investigation, any detrimental information will become known as a result of this scrutiny. However, in the 1980s Pope John Paul II did away with the devil's advocate system.

It is still a good tool for negotiators. Being a devil's advocate (see glossary) is a way to give a reality check to the other side and point out flaws in its arguments or the downside of its proposals. By saying you are going to play the devil's advocate, you are not your own advocate. It is a wonderful convention because it does not appear that you are actually making the comments on your own behalf. By taking on the outsider's role, you can point out the flaws in the other side's case. It is a great device or foil because the other side cannot take offense. It is not you talking; it is the devil.

Script:

Let me play devil's advocate for a minute. If we were to agree to that, it would cost us ten times what we are paying now.

Let me play devil's advocate. There are many downsides to that proposal.

Let me play devil's advocate. Even if you did all those things, the City Council is not going to approve it.

Rule 25. Save face.

Saving face is a way to allow a person to get out of an embarrassing situation with his dignity and reputation intact. People don't like to admit they are wrong or look foolish, so if you can give that person a way out, you are helping him save face. This is the opposite of driving someone into a corner, which will make a person fight even harder. Giving someone a way out is a tradition in many countries. This can work in negotiations because it is a way to help the other side avoid embarrassment. It is often used in politics. Something is done so the president can save face and not be embarrassed. You are helping the other side look good, and, as a result, you may get some concessions.

It is also a way to be creative about a solution. For example, if you have a high-ranking employee who is not performing his job for some reason, you may want to demote him. However, this could be devastating to the employee's ego, so perhaps you suggest a lateral transfer and a different title so he can go into the other position with his dignity intact. In such a situation, the employee may be a better worker rather than be angry and mad about a demotion. However, don't expect too much if you help someone save face.

Script:

If we allow that employee to transfer rather than be demoted, he might be able to save face.

That was a really stupid comment. Let's let him save face by ignoring it.

Rule 26. Watch the other side's body language.

Watching someone's body language can tell you a lot about a person.

  A. Avoiding eye contact may be a sign of lying.
  B. Having temper tantrums may be an attempt to ambush the negotiations.
  C. Placing a hand on one's face may be a sign of frustration.
  D. Crossing one's arms and legs may show resistance to your proposals.
  E. Clenching one's jaw may be a sign of anxiety and stress.
  F. Standing or sitting straight with good posture may be a sign of confidence.
  G. Raised eyebrows may show surprise.

On the other hand, if the other side has a poker face, it may be hard to tell what she is really thinking. Be careful not to put too much stock into body language. The other side may be acting and trying to throw you off with its responses. Some may be unaware of the implications of their body language. Some expressions are reflexive so people don't have that much control. For example, when we are pleased, our pupils widen. It may be more important to look for changes in body language. If you are observing the other negotiator, then you will be able to tell when there is a shift in body language. If someone is suddenly alert, it may signal that he is really listening and ready to negotiate.

Be careful that you don't give anything away with your body language. Don't smile or gloat when the other side makes a mistake or offers you something you really want. Don't drum your fingers on the table when you are bored or upset. Remember, negotiations are a lot like the game of poker. Having a poker face that does not show your cards is the best approach.

Script:

When he does not look me in the eye, I think he is lying.

I can't tell if he is frustrated with our proposal or just tired.

I have a poker face so you don't know what I am thinking.

Chapter 4 | EXTREME TACTICS

This chapter lists a few tactics that I normally would not use in negotiations unless it was going very poorly, and I was willing to pull out all the stops. If you are dealing with a person with whom you have had previous favorable negotiations, you probably don't want to use these tactics. Also, if you are dealing with a person with whom you expect to have future negotiations, don't use these tactics.

Be cautious before using any of them, and be aware that they can backfire. If you are at a point where things could not get any worse, and you are ready to give up anyway, you might want to consider one or two of them. Another disadvantage is that by using some of these tactics, you might escalate the tension with the other side making agreement even more unlikely. Use them sparingly. I am also including these extreme tactics so that you will recognize them if the other side uses them against you.

Rule 27. Have a temper tantrum.

If you want to make a point, a deliberately-staged temper tantrum might fit the bill. What makes this effective is that it is unexpected. If done sparingly, you can show that you mean business and are not to be trifled with. It can also backfire. If the negotiation is particularly volatile anyway and the parties are already discourteous and rude, a temper tantrum is not going to stand out. If you do get angry, it should be on purpose and should be staged for effect. You should be like an actor in a play.

Generally it is better to be polite and charming, but not too charming or you will appear to be insincere. If you get angry, and it is not staged, then you will be out of control. As Shakespeare said in *As You Like It*, "All the world is a stage and all the men and women merely players." The whole negotiation process is acting to some degree. You do not want the other side to know what your position is and how you really feel. However, on rare occasions, you may feel that the timing is right to show anger. Just make sure that you are really acting and that you are in control.

When you are on your last nerve, and you are told your reserved hotel room has been given to someone else, that controlled anger may be a way to get the hotel's attention since it won't want you to make a scene, especially in the lobby. On the other hand, you are always taking a chance that you will humiliate yourself. It is best to do this when you have nothing to lose and may never see this person again. Calculate beforehand whether the planned outburst is worth the risks. If you go forward, prepare your script and practice just as an actor would do. Give details so the person knows why you are so upset. Remember it has to be controlled, so don't go overboard with your performance. If you turn red in the face and start perspiring, your performance might have gone too far. When you do stage a scene like this, always end with a proposed solution. Otherwise your performance may be wasted, and the other party may not feel like proposing a solution after you have yelled at him.

What if the other side has a tantrum? The downside of you having a tantrum is that the other side may feel that it can have a tantrum, too. If the other side has a tantrum, ask what it is proposing? If a solution is not presented, then the tantrum won't have any impact. Don't get sidelined or intimidated by a tirade. Keep on track. Your job is to get the dispute resolved and everything else can be considered a diversion.

Script:

I have really had it to here! You want to know why I am mad! I am going to tell you!

I cannot believe that you would suggest such a thing! However, I do have a solution.

Having a tantrum is not going to resolve anything! Give me a solution or let's move on.

Rule 28. Walk away.

Sometimes you may feel that if you don't get what you want, you are ready to walk away. If you use this tactic in the negotiation process, use it sparingly. For example, if you want to make a point about the other side's behavior or tactics, you may want to say something strong and leave the room. Remember, if you do get mad (see Rule 30 above), it should be staged. You don't want to really lose control. If you fly off the handle every time something goes wrong, you will be crying wolf, and the tactic will be ignored.

For example, you might decide that you are going to ask for a raise or a promotion, and you are prepared to quit if you don't get it. Be careful when making this kind of gesture. You don't want to quit your job just because you lost your temper. You may want to resist that urge to go into your boss's office but, instead, go home and sleep on it. There are other ways to negotiate a raise that don't have the dire consequences of losing your job. On the other hand, if you are testing the waters to see if you can get an increase at your current job, that is a different situation.

When I was a director of human resources and someone threatened to quit, I would put a piece of paper in front of him and ask him to write "I resign" and sign and date it before he changed his mind. If I wanted to keep the employee, I might want to try to work something out.

Don't bluff if you are not prepared to take the consequences. Don't say you are going to quit if you are not willing to follow through. You will lose any negotiating power you have if you come back the next day begging for your job back.

Script:

You are not giving me much choice. If I must choose between giving you a promotion and you leaving the firm, I will have to choose that you leave.

You are a good employee, and I don't want to see you leave. Why don't you come back tomorrow so you can tell me why you think you deserve a raise?

Rule 29. Do not overreach.

Overreaching is a form of "dirty tricks." Here are some of the synonyms for overreaching: circumvent, frustrate, deceive, dupe and mislead. You can see why it is generally not a good idea to overreach. If you use ruthless tactics such as an ambush to annihilate the other side, the other side will want to retaliate against you at the next negotiation session or even sooner. You may have won the battle but lost the war. You may have gotten some concessions for your side, but the relationship with the other side is now completely deteriorated and full of distrust. You want to get as much as you can in a negotiation, but there will be consequences if you go to extremes. If the other side is so beaten down and humiliated that it looks bad to its members, it will be looking for an opportunity to humiliate you as well. The consequences of overreaching might not be immediately apparent, but the other side will wait for the right moment to avenge its humiliation.

If you are negotiating with a bully who does not understand the concept of overreaching, you need to be aware that the other side wants what it can get without any concern for future negotiations. You may need to be resigned to the fact that the negotiations might not ever be resolved.

If you are the one who overreached, you might not want to wait for retaliation; go ahead and meet with the other side and repair some of the damage of your tactics. It is difficult to have a good working relationship after negotiations have gone bad.

Script

We don't trust you anymore or believe anything you say after you used your dirty tricks in the last negotiations.

I thought the negotiation was going well until we were ambushed. We were not expecting that. We will expect it next time, though.

Rule 30. Create a diversion such as a smoke screen, decoy, or red herring.

In the military setting, smoke is released to mask the location or movement of troops. In the negotiation setting, it is a way to deflect your true intent or mask what is important. A smoke screen is a diversionary tactic to take attention away from your main objective and give attention to something of little or no importance. This can backfire if the other side realizes you are just wasting its time.

A decoy or red herring (see glossary) is a tactic to mislead the other party and create a diversion. Of course, the origin of the *decoy* is duck hunting, but the origin of the term *red herring* is more obscure. Red herring was rubbed on hounds to protect the hunted fox or fugitives from being caught. The hounds will smell the herring rather than the scent of the fox or men. A red herring is essentially a false clue or phony issue that is used to distract the voters or negotiators from the real issues.

We see diversionary tactics all the time in Washington, D.C. All the public attention might be on a false issue while the Congress is working on an issue behind the scenes. The public's attention is diverted from an important one to one that is a red herring and is not important. When the parties get the action they want, they then withdraw the phony issue.

Script:

We know that the issue of seniority is just a smoke screen. You are really wasting our time. Let's get back to something that is important.

All that discussion about safety was just a red herring. I know what the real issue is.

Rule 31. Take it or leave it.

The take it or leave it approach was used in a famous labor case in the 1950s involving Lemuel Boulware, a vice president for General Electric. Mr. Boulware went through a process of determining what was best for the company and what it could afford and presented his first, last, and best offer as a package deal to the electrical union and basically said, "Take it or leave it." The court determined that this was not good faith bargaining because there was no give or take between the parties and no involvement by the union. This take it or leave it approach is now called Boulwareism (sometimes spelled Boulwarism), named after that General Electric vice president who first used it. This approach is not really negotiation, since one side is not involved. One side is saying, this is what we want (or are willing to give), and we won't take (or give) anything less.

This technique should not be used in negotiations today, especially at the start of negotiations. However, if you are at the end of a negotiation, it might be an approach to use if phrased correctly. Never say that something is your final offer unless you have nothing else to give, and you are already very near the end of the negotiations. Saying it this way is not an unfair labor practice since the parties have been involved in the give and take of negotiations. Never say this is the final offer unless you really mean it and are willing to walk away.

Script:

If you are saying take it or leave it, we will leave it.

This is not Boulwareism. We want to hear your reaction to our proposal.

Chapter 5 | How to Apologize Like a Pro. To Forgive is Divine.

Rule 32. Everyone makes mistakes. To err is human.

Things happen, and mistakes are inevitable. If you make a mistake, say as an online seller who sent the wrong item to a customer, it is much better to "fess" up and tell your customer as soon as possible. If she finds out herself, she will assume you did it on purpose. When a mistake happens, assume you are dealing with a difficult customer and do everything you can to satisfy your customer so that she does not have a chance to complain. Don't expect to make money on that particular transaction.

Recently we have seen many examples of horrible customer service. Who could forget the image of the elderly man being dragged off the plane even though he had already boarded the airplane with a valid ticket? Later we learned that the man suffered a concussion and broken teeth and was in the hospital for a few days as a result of the rough treatment he received. If the flight attendants had had authority to offer a much higher incentive for volunteers to take a later flight, this would not have happened. The airline seemed more worried about the cost to get volunteers to leave rather than the well-being of its customers. By trying to save a few thousand dollars, the airline paid a settlement of millions of dollars as well as creating a major public relations fiasco.

How can something like that be avoided? Remember the adage that the customer is always right? That applies to mistakes, too. If you make a mistake, do everything to rectify it as soon as possible. Money spent up front will more than pay for itself in the long run. The airline must understand that it is in

36

the customer service business and is not just in the business of flying people from place to place like luggage. I was not surprised to find out the President of the airline had formerly been the CEO of a railroad transit company that did not transport people.

Let's face it; mistakes are inevitable. To err *is* human. If you are on the receiving end of a mistake, this is a chance to be magnanimous and understanding. Always remember that the goal is to resolve the dispute. The sooner you put the mistake behind you, the sooner you can concentrate on the solution. Don't make the solution overly complicated or get too many people involved. If you sent the wrong item to the wrong person, don't expect a customer to send the item to a third party. It might be better to offer a refund at this point. Don't be overly concerned about making money on this one transaction either. You will lose money when a mistake is made, but you may be able to keep the customer if she feels she has been treated fairly. If not resolved satisfactorily, that person will tell many people about the incident and post negative photos and comments on Facebook and Twitter.

Script:

I just realized that I agreed to something in error. It is entirely my fault, but I will have to take that proposal off the table.

Thanks for admitting that you made an error. We all make mistakes; let's see how we can move forward to resolve this.

Mistakes happen. Let's not dwell on who made the mistake; let's concentrate on how we might correct the error and resolve this.

Rule 33. Be willing to apologize. To forgive is divine.

What is an apology? A good apology is when one party accepts blame and responsibility for one's actions and shows some kind of remorse or regret. Sometimes a party only wants an apology in order to resolve a dispute. It sounds like an easy way to settle a situation since no money is involved. However, that is usually not the case. An apology is in the realm of feelings and principles. For some negotiators, an apology is not in their vocabulary because they see an apology as a sign of weakness.

Why is an apology so important to some people? It is a way to get their respect, dignity and reputation back. An apology can be very satisfying especially if the other side feels that he or she has been vindicated.

A. Here are tips for a good apology:

1. *The apology must be heartfelt and not be given begrudgingly.*
If it is not sincere, the apology will make the situation worse. If a person cannot give a sincere apology, it is not worth the effort.

2. *An apology cannot be sarcastic.*
A sarcastic apology defeats the whole purpose of an apology; this is not a time to be sarcastic or flippant. An apology must be sincere.

3. *You cannot add a "but" to the apology.*
You can't say, "I am sorry, **but** it was really your fault." That isn't an apology. I once had a serious argument with a family member; the next morning she purportedly called to make an apology, but then she added all the things I did wrong to the end of the apology. She should have just said "I am sorry."

4. *A good apology accepts blame.*
As stated in Rule 3 above, people love being told, "you are absolutely right." An apology that accepts blame is more likely to be accepted. "I really goofed on this. I am sorry and will try to make it up to you."

5. *Keep it simple.*
It is enough to say "I am sorry." or "I apologize." The more you say, the easier it is to get in trouble. Don't be tempted to add something more so that you make things worse.

6. *If someone apologizes to you, be gracious and accept it.*
It is hard for some people to apologize. Somehow it gets stuck in their craw. If someone apologizes to you, accept it, and move on.

7. *If you can't get an apology, then ask for money.*
If you are negotiating with someone who refuses to apologize, you may be able to get more money to settle the case. "All I wanted was an apology. Since you won't agree to that, then I want you to reimburse me for all the expenses I incurred to get this fiasco sorted out."

B. Here are some examples of weak and then revised apologies:

1. *I am sorry if what I said hurt your feelings.*

Translation: I am not really sorry for what I said, but I am sorry you took it the wrong way.

Revised Apology. *I am sorry I hurt your feelings.*

2. *I am sorry if I made a mistake.*

Translation. I am not saying I made a mistake but "if" I did, I am sorry

Revised Apology. *I am sorry I made a mistake.*

3. *I am sorry you were offended by what I said.*

Translation. I am not saying I am sorry I said it.

Revised Apology. *I am sorry I said that.*

4. *I am sorry if you misinterpreted my meaning.*

Translation. I am not sorry. You made the mistake.

Revised Apology. I am sorry I said that.

5. *I am sorry you didn't read the instructions.*

Translation. It's your fault for not reading the instructions.

Revised Apology. I am sorry the instructions were not clearer.

6. I am sorry we had a communication problem.

Translation. It's mostly your fault.

Revised Apology. I am sorry I misled you.

7. I am sorry that you feel that you need an apology for what I did.

Translation. I am not really sorry. You are very needy.

Revised Apology: I am sorry for what I said.

8. Quit pouting and come to the family reunion.

Translation. You are acting like a baby.

Revised Apology: Come to the family reunion.

Never underestimate the power of an apology. Remember "To forgive is divine."

Chapter 6 | CLOSE THE DEAL

After you have been negotiating for a long time, it can get frustrating and tiring when the negotiations go on and on, and nothing seems to get resolved. Sometimes the negotiations even start to unravel. Here are some rules to help close the deal.

Rule 34. *The devil is in the details.*

Even when there is preliminary agreement, be sure that all loose ends are tied down. Try to anticipate any contingency so that negotiations don't break down at a later time. It is easy in the excitement of resolving a long and complex dispute to stop the negotiations when there seems to be initial agreement and put off writing down the details. If you are too tired to continue, at least prepare a draft with all the details to bring to the next meeting. That initial excitement can get deflated when one party comes back the next day and says that the written document does not reflect the agreement. If you are caught in this situation, try to force yourself to write a clear and accurate statement of the agreement as soon as possible. Jot down everything you can remember as soon as you can after the meeting. Otherwise, it is easy to forget some of the details.

Although you may feel that one person is being a real stickler and very annoying, try to be patient. If the other side says it is important, try to work something out so the negotiations can be finalized. If the other side wants a solution for every possible contingency, it can easily bog down the process. Sometimes you have to agree in "principle" and leave the details to another day. It is a good thing to get all the i's dotted and the t's crossed. It is better to have any misinterpretations cleared up now rather than later. You don't want a grievance to be filed because a misplaced comma changed the whole meaning of a sentence.

It is a real balancing act. One one hand, you don't want to work on endless contingencies if none are likely to occur, but on the other hand, you don't want the language to be ambiguous or unclear as to the intent of the parties. At some point you need to say this is as far as we can go. One way to compromise is to work on the one or two contingencies that are likely to occur, not multiple ones that are not likely to concur. You don't want to waste a lot of effort on something unlikely to occur.

Script:

This is an important item, and the language must be exactly right in order for me to approve it. We must have all the t's crossed and the i's dotted.

Since we do not have time to work out all the details, let's write down the areas where we agree so we can work on this next time.

I know it is important to work out contingencies so we don't come back to the bargaining table. However, let's work on the one or two that are most likely to occur.

Why spend a lot of time on something that probably will never happen?

Rule 35. Trade-off or split the difference.

A trade-off is sometimes called a *quid pro quo,* which is Latin for *this for that.* It means that if you give me what I want I will give you what you want. We use the trade-off in everyday negotiating. We will eat Mexican food, your favorite food, tonight and then we will eat Japanese food, my favorite food, tomorrow. It is natural to say that if you give me this, I will give you that. It seems fair, and it is a way to compromise without giving up that much because you are getting something back in return. If you can trade something, you don't even want, that is even better.

Splitting the difference is a good strategy to use, especially near the end of negotiations. If you feel some momentum, and the parties are weary, that is the perfect time to suggest that since you are so close on a particular point, why don't we just split the difference? This won't work if you are very far apart. It can work if you are willing to compromise to finish the negotiation on a particular provision or complete negotiations altogether. Splitting the difference works best when a dollar amount needs to be negotiated. If the numbers are close, then bridging the gap makes sense. "You are at $200. I am at $100. Let's just split the difference at $150.

Script:

I am willing to do a trade-off. I will delete this provision if you delete that provision.

We are so close to the dollar amount. Why don't we split the difference and call it a day.

Rule 36. Step back and look at the big picture.

During dispute resolution, we are looking at the small picture. We are dealing with the facts and details of a dispute that are important to the parties, but they are usually not earth-shattering to anyone else. It is important to step back once in a while and see where the dispute is in relation to the big picture of your life and world events, Some people can get really wrapped up in whether the dispute is resolved and have a lot of frustration and anger. When weighed against world peace or global warming, it just loses its significance. If the case is not resolved, or you feel that you gave up more than you wanted, it does help to step back and look at the big picture. Sometimes doing this makes you take yourself less seriously. The other benefit is that sometimes you realize that this is the time to throw in the towel and close the negotiations.

Script:

I have worked long and hard on this negotiation. However, if we don't resolve it, it won't be the end of the world.

Let's try one more time to see if we can resolve it, and if we can't, let's call it quits.

Rule 37. Know when to hold and when to fold.

An impasse occurs when the parties are deadlocked, and there does not appear to be any room for agreement. You have come to a point where both parties are ready to give up. At this point there are a few strategies that might help to chip away at the impasse. If emotions are high and both parties are clearly frustrated and tired, it might be time for a break. Try to clear the air and get a fresh start the next day or the next week.

When you get back together, this is the time to emphasize mutual interests and stress the cost of not agreeing. This might also be a time to try to agree in principle and work out the specifics at a later time. It is also a good time to brainstorm to discuss solutions without making any decisions or commitments. Even a funny story can help relieve the tension of the deadlock. Asking *what if?* questions can also help show the consequences of not getting an agreement. Using a deadline might help, but be careful doing this unless you think that this will help move things along.

Just as the song says, you need to know when to hold and when to fold. Some things will never be resolved. When you have reached an impasse and have done everything you can think of to break the deadlock, it may be time to think of folding. If you have made several suggestions that were not met with any discussion or interest, this may be one of those disputes that doesn't get resolved. On the other hand, if you are moving very slowly but still making some progress, albeit at a snail's pace, it might be worthwhile to still plod away.

Not only is it important to know when to close the deal, but it is crucial to know how to close the deal. Otherwise a negotiation can go on and on and never get resolved. You may want to suggest a package deal to wrap things up. If you have nothing more to give, you need to tell the other side that there is nothing else to squeeze from you.

Script:

I would not say this is my "final" offer, but we are getting very close to it.

Let's take a weeklong break so we can look at this impasse with fresh eyes.

Let's take a look at what will happen if we cannot resolve this situation ourselves.

First, the decision will be out of our hands. Second, the employees will not get paid for at least six months. Third, neither party may get what it wants.

Can we put our differences aside and work out some kind of compromise?

We would like to take several items and make a package offer.

Honestly, we don't have anything more to give.

If we cannot break the impasse, then I suggest we close the case.

Rule 38. Follow up after negotiations

It is not over when the negotiations are over. The agreement still needs to be signed. In addition, followup may be needed throughout the term of the agreement. If it is a complex negotiation, you have probably kept drafts or notes throughout the negotiation and signed off on tentative agreements (see glossary, Appendix A) as they are agreed upon. However, it is important to look very closely at the finished documents and compare them to your notes and make sure that everything is as agreed. In addition, check very carefully for misspellings and typos. A misplaced comma or period could change the meaning of a whole section. There was a recent case where the lack of a comma cost a Maine company millions of dollars in overtime. I recently had a case as an arbitrator where the meaning of a comma in the collective bargaining agreement had to be arbitrated several years later. It is human nature to want everything to be completed in a hurry. However, this final review is of utmost importance, and this process is the one thing that should not be rushed.

Even if this was an informal negotiation, and you orally agreed, you should still put the agreement in writing. One way to do this is to write a letter to the other party to confirm in writing what was agreed and ask the other side to sign the letter, too. This should be done immediately so that the other party does not have a chance to change its mind. Even though it seems that both parties have agreed, sometimes the parties have a different understanding after it is reduced to writing.

You will need to review your signed document to see what follow-up is needed. There may be deadlines or contingencies in the agreement, so make sure that what is supposed to happen does happen. Other approvals may be needed before it is signed. For example, a union contract has to be ratified by the union membership. Sometimes, it must be approved by the city or county council in accordance to an ordinance. Then all the provisions need to be coordinated with the finance and human resources departments so that the wage changes are made in a timely fashion. Sometimes other provisions will be implemented in the second year or third of the agreement. Make sure there is a tickler file so all deadlines are met.

Script:

Let's write down what our agreement is so we can both sign it.

Let's review this document so there are no typos or mistakes.

In order for the implementation to be done on time, we will need to coordinate with the appropriate city departments.

Rule 39. Don't expect thanks or gratitude when it is all over.

After the dispute is resolved, move on. Don't expect any thanks or gratitude from the other party. The fact that the agreement has been approved is thanks enough. Don't expect the other party to be grateful that you spent so much time on the settlement or that you gave in on main points or that you gave a profuse apology. Sometimes there is a mental letdown when you have emotionally invested your energy in a dispute. You may have had some sleepless nights as you fretted about the pros and cons of your strategies and arguments. However, when it is over, let it go. Even though you should not expect thanks or gratitude for your efforts, you can still thank the other side for its efforts. Don't forget to thank your team for all the hard work they did. This good feeling might help future negotiations run more smoothly.

Script:

Both sides have spent a lot of time on this negotiation. I really appreciate the contributions you have made and the effort to resolve this dispute. Thanks.

Even though we got no thanks from the other side, that is not going to stop me from thanking them.

I want to thank everyone on our team for doing an awesome job. You are the best! We couldn't have settled this without you!

Chapter 7

How to Resolve Disputes with Difficult People (NEW CHAPTER)

Rule 40. You Can Negotiate With Difficult People

As I looked for topics to add to the third edition of *How to Negotiate Like a Pro,* I was getting a lot of questions and comments at book signings and festivals about negotiating with difficult people, specifically liars, narcissists and bullies and negotiators who were unreasonable, unpredictable and unprepared. I decided to devote a full chapter to this topic and outline techniques for various types of difficult people. Whether the other side is crazy or just temperamental, it is still possible to get a settlement although it may take a lot longer.

Here are some of my techniques.

1. *Don't let the other side's behavior get "under your skin."*
Be totally focused so that the other side's behavior does not get "under your skin" or that the other side does not get "into your head" as they say. The best way to respond to someone who says something totally absurd or ridiculous is to ignore it. It may be logical to the other side in some way, but usually I am not going to dignify the craziness by arguing against it. Usually I don't tell the person how ridiculous his claim or counteroffer is because it may needlessly offend him. Instead I push ahead and try to point out what I am willing to pay and ask if there is anything else he wants.

2. *Let the other side rant but make it a short rant.*

If the other side rants or otherwise wants to go off topic, I will allow it, up to a point. A healthy amount of venting can go a long way. Then if the other side is in a "take it or leave it" mode, I will try to frame my offers or plans in a different way using different words or phrases. I will try to give a rationale for my offers. I am reluctant to argue something that is patently absurd. I will just say. "That's impossible." or "I can't agree to that." and let it go at that.

3. *Suggest a break if the negotiations are heated,*

When discussions get emotional or irrational, suggest a long break or, better yet, an adjournment until the next day if time allows for it. Sometimes the other person is in a better or different frame of mind at the next meeting. Some negotiators seem to do better in the morning and others late in the afternoon.

4. *Schedule sessions near lunch time or near the end of the day*.

Some negotiators get peckish when they are hungry. Many cases have settled because it was close to lunch time or the work day was ending. Nothing like stomach rumblings or rush-hour traffic to make both parties much more amenable to resolving that last issue.

5. *Try humor*

Everyone can use a good laugh and humor can deflect rising tensions in a negotiation. Humor can also backfire so be careful with the jokes in case they could offend someone and make the other side angrier.

6. *Declare an impasse*.

If it is obvious that the other side is playing a game and has no intention of resolving the dispute, then declare an impasse. If the other side prefers to rant and rave rather than working on a solution, then at some point, you need to go ahead and declare an impasse.

A. How to Negotiate with a Narcissist

What is *narcissism? (see glossary, Appendix A)*. In Greek mythology, Narcissus, known for his great beauty, saw his own reflection in a pool and fell in love with it, not realizing that it was only a mirror image. He was so in love with his image that he lost his will to live and stared at the reflection until he died. Narcissus is the origin of the term *narcissism*. Here are synonyms for narcissists: arrogant, boastful, egocentric, conceited, haughty, megalomaniacal, ostentatious, self-important, selfish and vindictive.

The key to negotiating with narcissists is that the negotiation is all about the narcissists. They lack empathy and don't care about you or your point of view. It seems counter-intuitive, but if the other side is a narcissist, this can actually be an advantage for you. The narcissist wants to win, so if you can make the narcissist a winner, you are halfway there. You have to learn how to frame your issues so that the other side sees it as a win not a loss. As long as he gets a win and he looks good, the subject matter itself is not as important. It is classic case of form over substance.

Tips for negotiating with a narcissist.

1. Compliment the other side constantly.
As my mother used to say, "you get a lot more flies with honey than vinegar." Basically if you want something, be nice and polite rather than rude. If the other side does or says something good or smart, give a compliment. It sounds basic, but a well-phrased compliment can go a long way for anybody but especially for a narcissist. Try it out slowly and see where it goes. Don't be too fawning and when you get a compliment, make a big deal about it.

2. Leave your ego at the door.
Your intent is to make the other side look good. That may mean that you may have to look bad. It is really like acting. Your role is to make the other side look good no matter what transpires.

3. Be charming.
Be likable and interested in the other party. Ask questions and try to learn more about the other negotiator. Be good at small talk and ask about sports teams or hobbies. Stay charming no matter how the negotiation goes. Again this is an acting job.

4. Get to the point quickly.
Narcissists have short attention spans so get to the point quickly and don't make it overly complicated. Skip the background and history you might tell other types of negotiators.

5. Never interrupt a narcissist. It is always rude to interrupt anyone but interrupting a narcissist can be very offensive to the narcissist. However, don't be offended if a narcissist interrupts you because narcissists think that what they have to say is more important than what you have to say.

6. Find out exactly what the narcissist wants.
Ask what the narcissist wants. Try to get as much detail as possible.

7. Determine what you need to get in order to give the narcissist what he wants.
Figure out how you can accommodate the narcissist and still get what you need. When you make the offer, explain it in its best light to show how it is a "win."

8. Summarize.
A narcissist has a short attention span so summarize your points and have everything on one page if possible.

9. Prepare a written settlement beforehand.
This can save time later if the parties are able to reach agreement. Once you have a tentative agreement, urge the narcissist to sign. If you delay signing, the narcissist may change his mind.

10. If the narcissist balks at signing the agreement, see if he will sign it "in principle."
Sometimes one side wants every contingency written out before signing. If you feel you might be missing an opportunity to close the deal, you can suggest signing in "principle" which means that you agree generally to the provisions and commit to work out the details later.

11. Allow the narcissist to take credit for resolving the dispute,
Even if you deserve all the credit for getting the agreement settled, let the narcissist gloat and take credit. It is a small price to pay for a signed agreement.

12. Have a celebration at the signing of the agreement.
A narcissist loves a celebration, especially if he is the guest of honor. Take pictures, make a speech and serve champagne. Let the narcissist take a victory walk. Don't get in his way. This is a time for you to be humble and let the other side gloat!

B. How to Negotiate with a Pathological Liar

Pathological liars (see glossary, Appendix A), also known as *compulsive liars,* have a long history of lying and they lie all the time about everything. They don't need a reason for lying and sometimes they don't even realize they are lying since it comes so naturally to them. They don't understand the consequences of their lying either. Since negotiations are supposed to be based on trust, negotiating with a pathological liar makes negotiations very difficult.

Tips for negotiating with a pathological liar

1. Tell the truth.
Even when those all around you are lying, be sure you are telling the truth. Don't make things worse by lying yourself.

2. Ask a lot of probing questions.
Sometimes a person does not lie outright, but on the other hand, he is not forthcoming about something he seems to be hiding. Try to guess what he is hiding and ask some questions about it.

3. Assume the person is lying and look for inconsistencies.
Although you are assuming the other side is lying, analyze his version of the story and see whether there are inconsistencies. Ask questions about the inconsistencies and see if you can get to the truth.

4. Ask rapid-fire questions.
One technique is to ask rapid-fire questions so the other side does not have time to think about the lie and may actually tell the truth. At a recent hearing, a Cabinet Official complained that the pace of the questions by a Senator made him nervous. Perhaps he was afraid he would inadvertently blurt out the truth, which might be inconsistent with an earlier statement.

5. Assume everything the liar says is a lie unless proven otherwise.
In a negotiation based on trust, one party usually assumes the other party is telling the truth unless proven otherwise. When you are negotiating with a known compulsive liar, you need to assume everything said is a lie and act accordingly.

6. Take detailed minutes of all negotiating sessions.

Since you are assuming everything said is a lie or will be denied later on, it is imperative that you have good records of your previous meetings. If both parties agree, you could record the meetings. If the meeting is recorded, be sure to be the side that is responsible for transcribing the minutes of the meetings. If you can't record, have someone take detailed minutes of the meeting. At the beginning of each meeting, pass around the transcription or minutes of the previous meeting for the parties to approve before going on to new business.

7. Get everything in writing

Have the other side sign any provision agreed to by both parties as soon as possible. Have a draft available at the meeting so it can be signed after both parties agree to it. This will make it difficult, but not impossible, to change his mind later on.

C. How to Negotiate with a Bully

We have all seen a bully in the school yard, but lately bullies have been in the workplace and politics. When I think of a bully, these are some of the words that come to mind: control, bluster, threatening, aggressive, hostile, intimidating, accusatory, annoying, harassing, insulting, discriminatory, impatient, and taunting. Physically a bully tries to be intimidating by shaking his fist or raising his voice. In some ways, the bully is a one-trick pony. Being a bully is the trick and there isn't much else. When she doesn't get her way, she plays the bully role and tries to intimidate the other side.

Tips for negotiating with a bully.

1. Stand up to the bully and be confident.

People don't like being around bullies. They aren't very nice and they try to intimidate people. They make inappropriate comments and make fun of things that are politically incorrect. Why do they act like this? Probably because they can get away with it. If someone yells back at them, then they will yell back even louder.

Standup to the bully. Do not let him (or her) get to you. By standing up, I don't mean that you should try to intimidate him or that if he yells at you,

you are going to yell back at him. You are way too smart and dignified for that. My version of standing up is to hold your head high and ignore the bully tactics, even to the point of nonchalance. You may need to practice in front of the mirror to get the right nonchalant expression for your entrance, but the look I am talking about is efficiency with a little indifference. When I want to emphasize my self confidence, I always wear my red suit since red is supposed to be a power color. I suggest that you wear your power color whether male or female and make an entrance with enormous self-confidence.

2. Out-prepare the bully

As discussed before, negotiations are about being prepared and being over-prepared. Do your research and figure out your positions and come up with some strategies to figure out what the bully is trying to get from the negotiations. Draft your resolutions, prepare your backup plans, and memorize your talking points. Try to predict what the bully's goals are and what will be his objections to your proposals.

3. Find out what he wants

You can start off by asking him and perhaps he will tell you. You may have to figure it out indirectly. Once you have figured out what the bully wants from the negotiation, then you might catch him off guard by giving him a bargaining chip but first tell him what you want in order to be willing to make that first move.

4. Beat him at his own game. Expect the worst but hope for the best

If the bully starts being a bully and raises his voice or tries to threaten the negotiations, have a couple of zinger questions to ask him to catch him off guard. For example. If he is acting out, don't show your frustration or exasperation because that is what bullies want you to do. Just ask him pleasantly, "Why do you act like this?" or "Why did you bother to come to negotiations today if you aren't going to participate?"

5. Offer Plan B or Plan C

See if you can get some agreement and build on it. Propose your provisions and explain why you think it is good for both parties and how it will make both parties look good,.

6. Leave your ego at the door.

If there is any interest in pursuing any proposals, give the bully the credit and see if you can get some closure. Praise the bully and show him how agreeing to the solution is a win-win for both parties. Even if it was your idea, always give the credit to the bully and praise him for resolving a problem.

7. If the bully continues his intimidation techniques, take a break.

If the bully continues to try to intimidate in an appropriate manner, give him an ultimatum, but say it pleasantly. You could start with taking a break. Tell him that you find his behavior intolerable and that you would like to start fresh in the morning to see if you can reach some agreement.

8. Give him one more chance, then walk away.

Don't make concessions and don't give in. If the negotiations are getting nowhere, tell him that you will walk away because it's a waste of your time to pursue any more negotiations unless both sides are willing to discuss the issues. If he shows some interest in pursuing mutual concerns, then continue and see if you can get a contract. If not, declare an impasse and walk away.

Negotiating with bullies is difficult. You don't want to be intimidated, but you don't want to miss out on an opportunity to reach agreement if that is possible. Once you can crack that bully facade and get some work done, you could be on your way to agreement. Sometimes a bully does not want to resolve a dispute; he only wants to assert his dominance. Your job is to give the bully some opportunities to discuss the issues. If the bully doesn't want to discuss the issues, continuing the negotiation is pointless.

D. How to Negotiate with Unethical People

When you are setting the tone for the negotiation, you want to be known as fair and honest. As a negotiator, you should not compromise your ethics. Whether you are a professional negotiator or negotiating with your family or at work, it is always important to keep your reputation intact.

If you are not sure whether something is unethical, ask the following questions. 1. Would your mother approve? and 2. Would you feel comfortable if your actions or comments were a headline in your local newspaper?

If your mother would not approve or you would not like to see that headline in the local paper, then your actions are probably unethical. This is assuming that your mother, like mine, was very ethical. It is always better to err on the side of being ethical or honest. Even if something has the appearance of being unethical, don't do that either. Remember that once something happens to mar your reputation or credibility, it is very difficult, if not impossible, to ever get it back.

What if the other side is unethical? What if you were negotiating with Kim Jung-il for the release of American prisoners? Everyone knows that North Korea is a cruel regime and its leader is unethical. These kinds of negotiations are very difficult and take a long time because the risks are so high. You would be dealing with someone who does not obey the norms and cannot be trusted. Remain ethical no matter what. It is not a time to take short-cuts.

Tips for negotiating with an unethical party.

1. Record the meeting.
Taking minutes when the other side lies or is unethical creates a record to prove what was said. If the meeting cannot be recorded, take careful notes of what was said and circulate the minutes at the next meeting to be approved. A separate person, not the chief negotiator, should be responsible for taking the minutes.

2. Don't go to a meeting alone.
Always bring a third party to any meeting. Tell the third party to take notes and if that is not possible, write down contemporaneous notes as soon as the meeting is over. We have seen similar scenarios with former FBI Director James Comey when he met with President Trump one on one. He wrote a memo to the file right after he left the meeting and told others about it extemporaneously so he could prove what was said at the one on one meeting.

3. Be willing to walk away.
If someone does something that you think it is unethical, you must be willing to walk away. Compromising your ethics is not a good reason to stay in a negotiation.

Rule 41. Be ethical and don't make promises you can't keep.

4. It is very important not to promise something and later change your mind. Whether it is intentional or unintentional, it is still unacceptable. Promising something that you know you cannot deliver is dishonest and unethical. Usually this happens when one side gets caught up in the moment and blurts out an acceptance.

5. Be careful about agreeing to anything without proper authority.
Sometimes the negotiator does not have the authority to give something but somehow agrees to it anyway, knowing that the principal will probably veto his agreement. He gets caught up in the moment. It is much less embarrassing to take a break and call your principal to see if he agrees or to wait until the next day so you will have the time to discuss the proposed agreement.

6. Take safeguards if you know the other side is unethical.
Each step has to be confirmed. Remember the movie Bridge of Spies where Tom Hanks negotiated the release of a U-2 Spy Pilot? It was good theatre because we did not know if he would meet all the conditions and be released. You need to build in more safeguards and steps that can be verified to know that all agreements are being enforced.

7. If you make a mistake, tell the other party as soon as possible.
Sometimes at the end of a negotiation, momentum develops so that both sides are eager to resolve all issues. During this crucial time, it is easy to agree to something one party may later regret. However, mistakes do happen, and if you know that you cannot keep your promise, break the news as soon as possible to the other side. Apologize and try to move on with the negotiation.

Chapter 8 | NEGOTIATING ON THE PHONE OR ONLINE

Special rules apply when negotiating on the telephone or online.

A. How to Negotiate on the Telephone

When negotiating on the phone, you cannot see the other side's facial expressions or body language unless you are using FaceTime, Skype, or a similar service. You are dealing solely with a voice. You can use this to your advantage. If you come to an agreement, it is a good idea to send an e-mail or letter to the other side confirming what was said. When dealing with customer service representatives on the telephone, it may take a long time to get to a human being and even more time to talk to a person who has authority and is willing to help you resolve your problem. Any call can turn into a negotiation. For example, someone might call you and ask you how much you want for something or how much you charge for a service. When you are on the phone, it is easy to blurt out a number that you may later regret as being too high or too low. Even though you are on the phone, you can still say that you need to think it over and will call back later with your response.

Tips on negotiating on the phone.

1. Set the tone

You only have your voice in a phone negotiation so it is extremely important to literally set the tone. Modulate your voice and try to sound very professional. Be courteous when you call and try to control any frustration and anger. Don't let your voice tone give your position away. Don't make any sounds that sound as though you agree as you might in a personal call. Don't talk too

57

fast or too slow. Be calm and don't let your emotions manifest in your voice. Never raise your voice. It is not in your best interests to yell at the person who may be able to help you.

2. I need your help.

Say "I need your help" when you first start speaking with a customer service rep. Give a brief (and I mean brief) summary of the problem and say again, "I hope you can help me resolve this problem," Why do I suggest this? You want to make the resolution of your problem a team effort. The person on the other end of the line holds the key to solving your problem so you want to make a good impression. If you are mad about what has happened to you, it may be tempting to start with a rant, but that is not going to get you anywhere. Even though the customer service rep works for the same company that made the mistake, she knows nothing about your problem. She is a clean slate and is being paid by that same company to assist customers. She wants to solve your problem and wants to solve it quickly. If you can develop some kind of rapport, the rep may try to help you and think of a solution outside of the box since she knows how the company works and you don't. When the customer service rep first talks to you, be sure to get all her information, her company ID, her name, her telephone number and mailing address. If I get a customer service rep who does not seem helpful, sometimes I will hang up and call later with the hope that I get a more helpful rep on another call.

3. Prepare before you call.

A telephone customer service rep handles many calls and can be impatient if you are not articulate about exactly why you are calling and what you want. Make notes before the call so you know exactly what you are going to say. Since you are on the phone, you can even read your notes. Say exactly what you want. Maybe you want a refund or maybe you want a new item because your item is defective. Be clear as to what you want, and tell the rep why you want it. If a complaint file is opened, ask for the case number and the name telephone number and email address of the rep so there is some proof of the call.

4. Ask questions.

Sometimes the customer service rep assumes that you know its customer service policies and procedures. Ask them, "How can I get a refund?" or "How can I get a new item?" If they talk about their procedures, ask them for a copy so you can read them, too.

5. Only negotiate with someone with authority.

The person who answers the phone will often not have any authority to give you what you want, especially if you are asking for an exception to a policy. If the rep admits that only a manager can do that, then immediately ask to speak to the manager. If the rep says the manager is on another line, say you will wait for the call to end. See if you can get the name of the supervisor so you can call back if you get disconnected. When you ask to speak to a manager, try not to be insulting. Otherwise, you may be directed to the wrong person.

6. Be persistent.

Even when you are told that something cannot be done, be persistent. If you are not speaking to the supervisor, ask for the supervisor. If you believe you are getting nowhere, ask for the address of the president or customer service manager to contact so you can continue the discussion with someone else. Send all correspondence directly to the President and copy as many people as you can. It is unlikely that the President will answer, but someone else may answer because she is concerned that the President might see the letter. You can often find these addresses online even if the customer service rep is not helpful.

7. It doesn't hurt to ask.

Asking for something on the phone may seem more difficult than asking in person since you cannot interact directly with the rep. However, if you are speaking to a hotel or airline that gave you bad service, do not be afraid to ask for a free flight or a free hotel room or an upgraded flight or hotel room. Many of the chains are customer-service oriented, and some companies, such as Nordstrom, empower its employees to make their own decisions as to how to provide good customer service. Even if there isn't a problem, ask for something if it is more convenient. I once made a reservation for a suite to accommodate five people. It turned out there was only one bathroom and I asked if it would be possible to get two adjoining rooms instead, which they did at no additional cost. Companies are very aware of Trip Advisor and other rating services and can be more accommodating in order to get good ratings.

8. Keep track of the paperwork.

Keeping track of the paperwork is always important, but it is especially important when you are on the phone. That person on the other end of the line can easily be lost forever if you do not get the contact information at the beginning of the call. That is a good safeguard in case the connection is lost. Get the rep's correct telephone number, especially if you were transferred two or three times. You need to keep track of all calls with the customer service rep's name, number, telephone transaction number, e-mail, and postal address. In addition, write down everything that was promised. Send a follow-up e-mail or letter describing what was said, what was promised, and when it was promised. Getting this information and having a record will be useful if the rep does not do what was promised. At that point, go as high up the chain of command as you can with your complaint, including the company President.

B. How to Negotiate Online

Negotiating online has some fundamental differences from negotiating in person. First of all, it is not done extemporaneously; negotiations online are by definition a delayed process. One party sends an e-mail and then waits for a response. Like telephone negotiations, you cannot see the person, and in addition you cannot hear the person. You don't realize how much you rely on visual and audio cues until you communicate only via email messages. When we talk, we use inflection to indicate whether we are serious or trying to be funny. When negotiating online, you are getting all your cues from the online message. It is hard to get used to in the beginning, but in a way you cannot make any judgments about the person, and that is somewhat freeing.

Tips for negotiating online.

1. Follow email etiquette.

When typing emails, certain rules apply. Be careful with expressions like lol (laugh out loud,) smiley faces, funny noises, emoji's or anything else that might be amusing with your friends but not professional for an online negotiation. *Do not use ALL CAPS.* This is like shouting in a face-to-face negotiation and is considered very rude.

A joke or a funny remark may go flat when the other side sees it because the person cannot hear your inflection when reading it. The other side might even be insulted. Don't send large attachments that will take a long time to load and don't send lengthy messages that are difficult to read. Be careful of your tone. Somehow the cold language without inflection or visual cues accentuates the literal meaning of the language and sounds clinical. Be sure to have a greeting to give some warmth to the email.

2. Be careful with typos and misspellings.
Once an e-mail message has been sent, it cannot be taken away. Be careful with typos and misspellings. If your English is not proper, it can distract from your message. Because you are typing and thinking at the same time, it is easy to make mistakes that only get noticed after you have already sent your e-mail. That is why you should not send a message immediately after you have written it. Use spell checker and grammar checker. However, this is not fail-proof because you may have written a legitimate word, but the spell checker will not pick it up even though it is not the word that you intended. If your cell phone finishes your words for you, make sure it is the word you intended.

3. Negotiations online are more exacting.
In a face-to-face negotiation, the other side quickly forgets exactly what was said, but in an online negotiation, either party can go back and review all the emails and see exactly what was written. Therefore, it is important not to act hastily after receiving a message, especially if you are angry and want to send back a sarcastic e-mail. Go ahead and write it out, but don't send it yet. Sleep on it, and then review your e-mail the next day before you decide whether to send it or whether to tone it down. It is very important to proofread and double-check everything before it goes out. If you have read some of your e-mails after the fact, you know that it is easy to make typing mistakes, and they are not easily spotted when you first proofread it. Once you have sent it, it is too late. You can create more problems if you are dealing with damage control with an e-mail full of mistakes and typos. The other side can also be offended if the e-mail looks carelessly written because of all the grammar and spelling errors. It sets a tone that you don't care and are not professional.

4. Don't give anything away without getting something.
Now that you are sending messages via e-mail, don't forget that this is still a negotiation. Don't be lulled into forgetting some of the basic premises of negotiation such as not giving away something without getting something. It may be easy to chat online, but focus on your goal and use the same

negotiation techniques. You still need to get something anytime you give something away.

5. Don't rush or be too slow. Know the rhythm.

The rhythm of an online negotiation is very different from being in the same room. You have to set the pace. Don't be too slow by not answering the e-mails in a timely manner. If one party takes days or even weeks to answer an e-mail, it can make the pace so slow that the parties lose interest altogether. On the other hand, don't make it look as though you are waiting at your computer for the other side's next message. Even if you feel you are on a roll, wait some time between messages. You do not want to appear too eager. The other party may think that you are desperate to settle. Once you send some e-mails back and forth, you will develop your own online rhythm.

Chapter 9 | How to Negotiate in the Workplace

As employees, we negotiate our salaries, hours of work, vacations, training, promotions, and sometimes even our discipline and termination. As bosses, we negotiate with our employees to try to make them more productive. We work with them to do certain tasks and reward them with raises, promotions and benefits like health insurance. We discipline them with demotions, suspensions, or even termination.

A. How to Negotiate salary.

You get the telephone call announcing that you have gotten the job. The employer is ready to make you a salary offer. What do you do next? First of all, you should keep in the back of your mind how important your salary is especially if this is your first job after college. That salary will follow you for the rest of your career. If you leave money on the table, say $2500.00, that can affect you for the rest of your career. Your salary increases and promotions are usually based on a percentage so compounding that $2500 over twenty or thirty years can make a big difference.

1. Get the employer to make the first offer.

This can be a little tricky, but try to get the employer to make the first offer of salary. Why is it so important for the company to make the first offer? The answer is simple. You do not want to leave any money on the table. Let's say you are willing to accept $90,000 for this position although you are hoping to break $100,000. Once you say the salary that you will accept, you can never go higher than that figure. If you said you would accept $90,000, and the employer was going to offer you $95,000, you have already lost $5,000. If the employer goes first and offers you $95,000, you are already ahead $5,000 and maybe you can get a higher offer by the end of the negotiations. Doing so can be a great advantage in getting the highest salary possible.

2. Be mindful of your salary requirements throughout the process.

For example the job application may ask you what your salary requirements are. Try not to give a specific amount, but if you must, make it higher than what you think you can get. A better answer is to give a range. If you are hoping to make $100,000, give a range of $100,000 to $120,000. If you are already familiar with the company's pay ranges, say that you want to be in the upper part of the appropriate range if you have the requisite experience.

3. Online application.

Sometimes the online application won't let you write anything other than a number. In this situation, you should put something high enough so that you could accept it but not too low so that you will wonder if you left money on the table.

4. Answer a question with a question.

If the employer asks you during the interview, "What are your salary requirements?" answer the question with a question since you don't want to give a salary offer first.

    A. How much is budgeted for this position?
    B. What is the range?
    C. What is the top of the range?
    D. What does the job description say?

5. What is the range?

If the employer answers, "The range is $75,000 to $100,00;"
then you can answer, "the top of the range." This can be a cat and mouse game, but don't take it too far or you might annoy the employer.

6. Most employers expect you to haggle over salary.

However, there is usually more flexibility in the private sector than in the public sector, which often has special rules on the starting salary and how it fits into the salary ranges. Be sure to get a copy of the personnel policies and the salary plan.

7. Never accept the employer's first salary offer.

As tempting as the employer's first offer may be, do not accept it right away. Say that you need a day or two to think it over and discuss with your family. Most employers understand that you need some time. No matter how high the offer is, chances are you may be able to get a little more. Remember, the company would not have made you an offer if it did not want you to accept it. You are the top candidate, and it wants to hire you. This extra time will also give you some time to research what other companies are paying and the cost of living in the area if you haven't already done this. After you have thought about the salary, go back to the employer and ask for $5,000 more or some amount with which you are comfortable.

When you get a new job at a new company, your old salary, is usually used as a base for the new salary. If it is deflated because of poor negotiating, you will feel the results for a long time. On the other hand, if you negotiate a good first salary, that is a gift that keeps on giving throughout your career! Keep this in mind before accepting the salary. There are exceptions to every rule. Once I got an offer so high that my brother-in-law said, "Mary, you better accept that offer before the employer revokes it." I did accept it and found out later that I was close to the top of the range anyway.

8. Give some rationale for the proposed increase in salary

A. My current salary is higher than that.
B. The cost of living is higher here than where I am living.
C. The job duties are at a higher level than my current job, but the salary is the same.
D. I will only be getting two weeks of vacation which is a 2 % decrease in salary.
E. I need a higher salary since you don't contribute to health insurance.
F. I would like to be reimbursed for my moving expenses.

9. Look at the employer's full benefit package before accepting the offer.

The total benefit package is much more than salary. Sometimes this is as much as 40% or more of the base salary. You should be thoroughly familiar with the total package before you make a decision. You may discover that your old position has a better package, or you may discover that even with a lower salary, you still have a better package with the new job.

A. Health insurance

Many employers are cutting back on health insurance, so you will need to find out if the employer provides health insurance and how much of the total premium it pays. You need to read the benefit booklet to see what the deductibles and co-pays are, so you can make a fair comparison. Many companies don't provide health insurance until you have worked sixty or ninety days at the new job. Be sure to be aware of what the policy is so you are not left without insurance during your first months of employment. Of course, this is a national topic and many drastic changes are occurring so you need to keep up-to-date and research this thoroughly. As we all know, healthcare is very complicated.

B. Vacation and sick leave

Many companies are offering PTO (paid time off) instead of a separate sick leave and separate vacation policy. If you are able to negotiate an extra week of vacation, that is equivalent to 2 percent of salary. Ask if employees are allowed to sell unused annual vacation if it is not used. Some employees want as much vacation as they can get, and others would just prefer the money.

C. Retirement benefits

Retirement benefits are being reduced by many companies. Find out if the company offers a defined benefit or a defined contribution plan. With a defined benefit retirement plan, you count the number of years times a multiplier, such as 2 percent, times the average of the top five years or salary, or something like that. Many police officers and teachers are under such a plan, which is often part of a collective bargaining agreement. Because of their expense and continued responsibility, many public employers are switching to a defined contribution. Defined benefit programs are less and less common, especially for new employees.

More common is the defined contribution plan where the employer contributes a percentage of salary and the employee may also contribute a percentage of salary to a plan, and the employee manages its investment. These are called 401A plans in the public sector and 401K plans in the private sector. Since so many employees lost so much money in 2008–09, many employees have postponed their retirement in hopes of recouping some of that money.

You need to also find out what the vesting period is. Usually there is a waiting period before you can get the retirement benefit. It can vary from one year to ten years. If you leave before the vesting period has vested, you will only get the investment from your own contributions.

D. Moving expenses

If you are moving from another area, you should ask for moving expenses. It is better to get the higher salary which includes your moving expenses. That will be a higher base for future increases. It is also more convenient since you won't need to deal with the paperwork of moving expenses reimbursements. You get the money up front. However, the employer may want to keep the base salary and reimburse you, up to a specific amount, for your moving expenses. Although this is not as good financially as paying moving expenses directly, it is a good alternative so that you can at least get your moving expenses paid. Either way make sure moving expenses are in your written offer.

E. Other Financial benefits of the position

You may want to factor in other employer-paid benefits such as travel expenses, conferences, and member dues

F. Other Factors

Although the following may not be deal breakers, you may want to ask them anyway:

1. How often are raises given? (six months or yearly?)
2. Is this an hourly position with overtime or a salaried position?
3. What are the work hours?
4. Where is your office?
5. Where do you park?
6. Does company have childcare for employees?

G. Is there something you want other than money?

If the employer has said it cannot give any salary higher than their current offer, is there anything else you want other than money? For example, do you like the title of your new position? Perhaps you could suggest a better title that better reflects your idea of the position.

10. Don't give notice at your old job until you have a written signed contract and have met all contingencies.

If you have a verbal agreement with your new employer, do not quit your job until you have a signed written contract. Some employees jump the gun and resign before they have that written contract. Some contracts have contingencies like a drug test or a background check. Wait until these are finalized before you resign. I have seen a few applicants fail one of these requirements and they are forced to go back to their old employer to see if they can rescind their letter of resignation, which, of course, can be humiliating. Sometimes, the old employer will say no especially if it has already filled the position with someone new.

One company I worked for had a no-smoking policy and applicants signed a sworn statement that they were non-smokers. We had an employee come to HR on her first day with cigarette breath and when asked she admitted she was a smoker. When she signed the sworn statement, she had intended on quitting before starting the new job. She lied on her application so suddenly she was without a job.

B. How to Negotiate With Your Boss

Negotiating with your boss can be a little tricky because you are not on an equal footing. It is even more difficult if your boss is a bully. Since there could be repercussions for speaking out, an employee usually won't tell his boss what he is really thinking. The basic difference between workplace negotiations and other negotiations is that employees are not equal partners in the negotiations. The boss usually has the upper hand because he also has the power to discipline or fire you. Be mindful of this disparity as you negotiate with him or her. You may be limited to what you can say or do.

Let's assume that you want to get a raise or a promotion. Here are some tips for negotiating with your boss.

1. *Don't be distracted by your emotions.*
If your boss has rejected your request for a raise or a promotion, do not let your emotions interfere with your response. If you are angry because you were passed over for a promotion or did not get the raise you think you deserved,

it is not a good idea to immediately go to your boss's office and demand a meeting. You will appear to be out of control, which you probably are, and the boss will probably be glad he made the decision he did.

2. *Research and prepare your response and rebuttal.*

The best thing you can do is use that energy and start writing down everything you would like to tell the boss about why you deserved the promotion or raise. Write down everything you can remember about what you were told that you had to do to get the promotion. Compile all records, such as letters, e-mails and a calendar or diary of your meetings, so you can review them and prepare the rebuttal for your boss.

3. *You don't have to like your boss to negotiate with her.*

It does not matter if you don't like your boss or if he is a bully and has annoying traits. It is unlikely that your boss is going to change or wants to change. However, you can still negotiate with your boss. You cannot let your dislike for your boss interfere with your request for a meeting for a raise or promotion. You need to separate the issue (the raise or promotion) from the person. It is also important not to assume the outcome is negative. Don't tell yourself, "What is the use? He does not like me, and no matter what I say, he is not going to change his mind!" That is self-defeating, and if you really believe that, there is no point in trying to change your boss's decision. You need to put your feelings about your boss aside and negotiate with him the same way you would if you liked him.

4. *Know what you want*

It is very important to know how much you want when you speak with your boss about a wage increase or any other benefit. If the boss asks you, "How much do you want? You need to have an answer rehearsed, This is not a time to hesitate. Be careful with the amount that you give him. Don't make it so little that you kick yourself later for not asking for more. Don't make it so much that the boss thinks you are greedy and unrealistic. If you're not sure, go for the higher amount. If you are asked why you deserve the raise, do not say, "I don't know." The answer needs to be rehearsed so that you can give a response anytime anywhere.

5. *Know what you are worth.*

Before you tell your boss how much you want, you need to do as much research as possible before the meeting. Find out what others in comparable positions are making at your company. This can be difficult in a private company but is usually available in the public sector. Each state's sunshine (open government) laws are different. For example, Florida's law is very liberal, and public salaries are available to anyone who asks the employer for this information. When you get the information, then you need to analyze it. For example, if the person you are comparing yourself to has five more years of service, then you need to factor that in. County or state information might also be helpful. It depends on the position itself. For a city manager salary, you would probably look at other cities in the county and other counties nearby of the same size. Read the employee handbook to see if there is a policy pertinent to salary review and evaluations. Be aware of time frames, requirements, and any appeal process, if any. You don't want to find out later that you missed a deadline.

6. *What is important to you may not be important to your boss.*

Your raise or promotion is very important to you, but it may not be that important to your boss. Having a meeting with you might be annoying, uncomfortable, boring, or even economically unadvisable. You are going to be well prepared for your meeting. However, your boss may not even have read your file, and, instead of thinking about your problems, he might be thinking about his career and his problems. He may have instructions from his boss concerning budget increases and may feel that his hands are tied regarding your situation. He may even agree that you deserve a raise, but he has to go with the party line. You need to be aware of these possibilities or distractions and not be flustered when your boss is not overwhelmed by your logic and knowledge.

7. If you don't ask, you don't get.

You may think that your employer is not going to agree to anything you suggest, but the worst thing he can say is no. You never really know until you ask, and you might be pleasantly surprised. You have nothing to lose, and the boss might appreciate your ingenuity or persistence. Some benefits you might request at work are telecommuting, an extended leave of absence, training courses, a new computer, a corner office, flexible time, extended hours, more work, less work, membership in a professional organization, or travel to a national conference. The list is endless and only limited by your imagination. However, don't overdo it so that you ask for something every time you speak with your boss. A good time to ask is when you have done well on an assignment.

8. *Be persistent.*

Your boss may tell you right away that you are not getting a promotion or a raise. If you accept that you are not getting it, then that is the end of the meeting. Perhaps you can suggest some alternatives. If you don't get the promotion, maybe you can at least get a raise. Ask for another meeting to discuss the issues raised. Ask if you can you get a provisional promotion, and if it does not work out, you will go back to your current job? Maybe you can assume the duties of the new position and postpone a raise for six months? Maybe you could ask for something else instead of a raise, such as extra vacation days or have expenses paid for a training conference concerning your new duties. As you can see, there are many possibilities. If you can suggest some to your boss, maybe one will stick. If your boss still says no, then you may have to go to Plan B.

9. *Have a Plan B.*

If you have your heart set on getting a raise or promotion, you still need to have a Plan B. First you have to decide whether you are going to stay in the position anyway or start looking for a new job if you don't get the raise or promotion. Even if you decide that you are going to look for a new job, don't be too quick to quit the old job.

If you decide to stay, whether permanently or while you are looking for a new job, you may want to look at your current job in a new light so that you can get more experience to help get the promotion next time or to get a new job. For example, you may want to consider taking classes to improve your skills especially if you have a tuition remission program. You may want to volunteer for projects at your company that are outside your field of expertise or comfort zone so that you can widen your experience on your resume.

Sometimes the Plan B is a lot harder to determine than Plan A. A lot of time and energy has been invested in moving forward in your company. When Plan A falls apart, it can be emotionally devastating. It is always good to have developed Plan B, C, and D just in case the others do not work out. When you are dealing with your livelihood, it can be very disheartening to try to figure out alternatives. If you have made a decision to leave the company, you should definitely know what Plan B is before quitting or threatening to quit.

10. Walk away.

There may be instances where you decide that you just have to walk away. If the boss is not willing to make you partner or give you the raise you thought you deserved, you may decide that this not the boss or company you want to work for anymore. Just make sure this decision is not made in haste while you are still angry about your boss's decision. If you do walk away, have a plan so you know how you will proceed. It is the conventional wisdom that it is harder to find a job when you no longer have one. Give yourself some time to make this final decision. You do not want to come into your boss's office on a Monday morning and beg for your job back. You would not be in a position of strength.

11. Step back and look at the big picture.

When you don't get an expected raise or promotion, it is a good time to reflect on the big picture. Here are some questions you might want to ask yourself. Your answers will help you decide the direction of your next move.

A. Can I stay here and work out these issues with my boss?
B. Or is this a good time to throw in the towel and go with another company or with another type of employment?
C. Where do I want to be five years from now or fifteen years from now?
D. Do I want to be self-employed, where I make my own decisions?
E. Was this really a blessing in disguise?
F. Am I better off knowing that this job is not for me so I can go in another direction with my life?

Chapter 10

How to Negotiate with a Difficult Spouse or an Ex-Spouse

It can be difficult negotiating with a current spouse because you will still be living with him or her after the negotiations are over. A certain amount of decorum and sensitivity is needed. Negotiating with an ex-spouse is more difficult because of the emotional stress. Most people don't like their ex-spouses; otherwise, they would probably still be married. The qualities they liked in their spouses may be the same ones they find annoying. Divorce usually brings out the worst in both parties. An otherwise rational wife or husband may act crazy, irrational, and petty during the divorce process. When children aren't involved, there is no reason to ever see each other again. However, when children are involved, it will still be necessary for the ex-spouses to be in contact and negotiate issues such as visitation and custodial support expenses at least until they are eighteen.

A. How to negotiate with a difficult spouse or significant other.

When you are negotiating with your spouse, there is a certain balancing act that is required. This applies to your parents as well as to your siblings. You can pick your friends, but your family is forever.

1. *Don't negotiate while angry.*
This is probably the most important rule for spouses. The best time to negotiate any important issue with a loved one is to negotiate when you are calm, cool, and collected. If you have just had an argument and are very upset or angry, this is not a good time to try to work things out. If you have had a few drinks, it is definitely not a good time to settle something. If you burst

into your home after a bad day and can't wait to tell someone off, this is not a good time to negotiate. You should wait a few hours or until the next day to have this conversation.

2. *Don't give an ultimatum.*

It can be tempting in an argument to say something like, "If you go out that door, don't come back!" or "If you don't like it here, just leave!" If you are having serious issues, which need to be negotiated, giving threats or ultimatums is not going to work. It puts the other person in a fight or flight position. If the spouse decides to stay, there can be a lot of resentment, and if the spouse leaves, that really does not resolve anything. If you think you may be headed for a divorce, this usually is not the way to resolve any issues. If there is some behavior you believe must stop in order to save the marriage, that, of course, needs to be discussed. This might be a good time to get counseling in order to have a third party give some structure to these discussions. If you feel you have to give an ultimatum, make sure that you have thought through all the consequences. For example, one spouse may give an ultimatum that the other spouse go into drug rehab before agreeing to move back to the marital home.

3. *Do not have a temper tantrum.*

As mentioned above, you should only use a temper tantrum if it is used sparingly and only when it is acting. It is a way to tell the other side that you are very distressed by what is happening, and usually the other side will take notice. However, if you routinely resolve arguments by having temper tantrums, this can get old in a hurry. This is like the children's story where the little boy called "wolf" so many times that when the real wolf came, no one believed him. When you are negotiating with a spouse, it is disrespectful to have a temper tantrum. Again, if you are feeling angry, postpone any negotiations.

4. *Have a Plan B.*

When negotiating with a spouse, it is very important to be flexible. Ask questions that start with *how?* or *what if?* This will help you come up with alternatives. *What if* you pick where we go on vacation this year, and I will pick next year? *What if* we go to a museum today and go to the racetrack tomorrow? How can I help you? How long do you think this will take? A relationship is all about compromise so come up with a plan B or even a plan

C or D so that you are making a good faith effort to get both parties involved in solutions.

5. *You don't have to be right to settle.*

We love to hear our spouse say, "You are right." It is even sweeter if our spouse says, "You are absolutely right." Many partners are constantly keeping score and say things like, "I knew that was going to happen." or "I knew I was right." It can be very disarming to tell someone that yes, you agree, she is right. This can stop someone in her tracks. What can you say to that? You almost have no choice but to move on. The alternative is to say, "You are dead wrong, and I am right." This just sets up a confrontation, and nothing is going to be accomplished. Try saying, "You are right," and see what happens.

6. *Don't overreach.*

Don't be smug if you get your way all the time. Even if it is not discussed, both parties are keeping score as noted above. If you always get your way, your spouse may be waiting for an opportunity to retaliate for all these small humiliations. Try to keep the scorecard relatively balanced. Let your spouse win an argument, or do what he or she wants with the understanding that next time you will do what you want. You may feel triumphant that you have proven that your spouse is wrong and that you are right and that you want things to go your way because you are consistently right. If you don't fight fairly, you may win the battle but lose the war. Your spouse may resent your tactics and no longer trust you. Fighting about these petty details can be exhausting, and just because you always win does not mean that the spouse isn't holding grudges, which may erupt some day.

7. *Write down your discussion points.*

I always find it helpful before a big discussion to write down all my arguments and discussion points. I take this very seriously and try to anticipate what the other person is going to say. I then write down my counterpoints to each argument. I then practice my arguments in front of a mirror so I am comfortable with what I am trying to say. I even take notes during our conversation. Formalizing the process works for me because I know what I am going to say.

8. *Save face. Don't make your spouse look bad*

Last but not least, don't make your spouse look bad. Try to make your spouse look good. If you back someone into a corner, it is human nature to try to fight back and try to retaliate. You never want to embarrass or humiliate your spouse. If she looks good, you look good as well.

B. How to negotiate with a difficult ex-spouse

It can be very stressful negotiating with an ex-spouse. Usually you are both on opposite sides of a solution. One or both parties may still have unresolved grudges or disappointments as a result of the divorce, and these can interfere in the negotiation process.

1. *Focus on the goal. Don't be distracted by emotions.*

Any meetings with your ex-spouse should have a specific purpose. It is very important to focus on your goal and not let your anger interfere with that goal. For example, let's say that you are figuring out a yearly schedule for vacations and weekends for your children and that you have already agreed each parent gets half of the holidays and half of the weekends. Your ex-spouse may try to bait you to get you off track and bring up some issue concerning the divorce or your past relationship. If you start to get distracted about something else, always come back to the goal of completing the schedule.

2. *You can negotiate with a difficult ex-spouse.*

Even if you don't like your ex-spouse and your ex-spouse does not like you, you can still negotiate with each other. It won't be easy, but try to set your animosity aside while working on joint issues. I like to take a few breaths before entering the room, and I say to myself, "I can do this."

3. *Look forward, not back. The past is called the past for a reason.*

Don't let past arguments enter into the discussion today. If your ex-spouse makes a snide remark or criticizes you, try to ignore it. You are meeting to discuss this year's calendar, not last year's problems. Again, you are focusing on the goal.

4. *Know what you want.*

Know in advance what weekends you want. Know all the dates you are requesting to have custody, vacations, birthdays, etc., and those days you don't care about custody because you are going to be away for business. Don't tell the other side yet what your preference is.

5. *Request ground rules.*

If previous discussions have been ugly, you may want to suggest some ground rules to make the process go more smoothly. For example, you may want to agree on the procedure for picking days. Do you go month by month or take turns picking days throughout the year? If you cannot decide on this in advance, it will be chaotic and take forever. You may want to have some ground rules for behavior, too. One person will be allowed to speak without interruption. There should also be rules for dealing with changes in the calendar during the year and the proper notification to the other spouse.

6. *Volunteer.*

You have to make a judgment call as to whether it is an advantage for you to do the first draft or for your ex-spouse to do one. Usually it is an advantage so this might be a good time to volunteer to do a first draft of the schedule. The other side may not want to take the time to do it. Expect lots of criticism. If you let the other side do it and there are problems, you can point out that it is his handiwork, and he signed off on it. This is your call. If you do it, you may be able influence the methodology of picking the days.

7. *Agree on the issues and prioritize them.*

You both need to prioritize your preferred days. If you do the first draft, you can recommend a system of taking each side's first priority and putting it on the calendar and then taking the other side's first priority. When there is an overlap, then you can have some discussion about deciding who gets the days. When there is discord, the more you can make automatic, the easier the negotiation will be.

8. *Anticipate what the other side wants.*

You need to anticipate what your ex-spouse wants. Since you lived with your spouse, you probably have an idea what he or she will want. You probably already know the birthdays or other important days. Try to figure it out as much as possible in advance so you can fit the anticipated dates into your schedule.

9. *Don't gloat.*

If you get something you want, don't gloat. There is nothing worse than seeing an ex-spouse gloat or smirk. Your ex-spouse will want to take that expression off your face and will try to retaliate. Go through these negotiations with a poker face.

10. *Trade off or split the difference*

There may be chances for a simple trade-off. You take that weekend and I will give you this weekend. You can agree to alternate holidays and birthdays. Don't expect the dynamics to be simple. When you do these trade-offs, don't make them unwieldy or inconvenient for your children. Remember that this should be for the benefit of the children. One day here and one day there just because their parents could not agree is not fair to the children.

11. *Watch the other side's body language.*

Since you lived with your ex-spouse, you should be able to read his/her body language. Use this information to your advantage. If you see that vein in his forehead bulging, you may know he is very upset. If she is thumping her fingers on the counter, you may know she is impatient and bored. Try to use these moods to your advantage. If he is mad, it might not be the best time to talk about the Christmas holidays. If she is getting impatient, maybe you can wrap it up.

12. *Don't expect thanks or gratitude when it is all over*

If you were the one who did the drafts and graphs and spent a lot of time on various drafts of the calendar, don't expect any thanks or gratitude. Just be glad the calendar is finished.

13. *Your lawyer is your backup plan*

My example of scheduling is a relatively simple problem Some problems can be very difficult for the parties to be in the same room to discuss. If this is the case, it may be worthwhile to have your lawyer talk to your spouse's lawyer so that you don't have to deal with your ex-spouse directly. It will cost you some money, but it will probably be worth it.

Chapter 11

How to Negotiate and Get Good Customer Service

In the news, we see horrible examples of customer service. Passengers get dragged off planes, and parents are told that their children will be put in foster care because they aren't following airline rules.

People feel entitled to rant and rave and cellphone cameras get photos of almost anything negative that happens. Customer service is very important to many companies today. Many want to exceed your expectations so you will become a repeat customer. These service companies may be receptive to negotiating with you. Other companies are not so enlightened or they have employees who are not given any leeway in their enforcement of company rules.

A. How to Negotiate with a Hotel

Negotiating with a hotel is usually not as emotionally charged as negotiating with your boss or spouse. However, if you have just had a long flight, and you come into a hotel and find that your reservation has been given to someone else, you will still be upset. These same rules would also apply to restaurants and most other customer service establishments. Here are some rules to use when negotiating with hotels.

1. *Do your research.*

When you call to make a reservation you should have already done your research. What is the rate online? What discounts can you use, AARP or AAA? Are there promotions? Are there special weekend or weekday rates? If you are a local getting hotel rates for family, ask if there is a neighbor rate. You should also look up the comparable rates of nearby hotels. You can go online and get reviews from other consumers or recommendations from guidebooks. How many stars does it have? Call more than once so that you can see if you get different quotes. If you get an offer online or on the phone that seems too good to be true, make your reservation immediately so that you don't lose the rate. Join a loyalty program so that you will be notified of specials and can use your points for free rooms. Be sure to note the time requirements for canceling your reservation just in case.

2. *Only negotiate with someone with authority.*
When looking for a good rate, it might be better to deal directly with the front desk instead of going online or through the hotel's website. Individual hotel managers often have authority to be more flexible in rates, especially late at night. The online rates usually cannot be altered. If you have a problem at the desk or while staying at the hotel, it is always a good idea to ask for the manager. Again, this may be the only person with the authority to give you something for your inconvenience, such as an upgrade or free room.

3. *If you don't ask, you don't get.*
When calling on the phone or asking at the desk, try to probe for a better deal. The associate usually won't offer one outright, so you need to ask the right questions. You could ask these questions: "Is that the best you can do?" "Do you have any specials?" "If you cannot lower the price, can you give me an upgrade?" Ask for a "neighborhood special" if you reside locally. If you don't ask, you don't get.

4. *Keep track of the paperwork.*
Once you get your reservation, make sure that you get your confirmation number, and the name of the person who made the reservation. You might want to call a few days later to make sure you still have that great rate. If you have problems at the hotel, keep copious notes of what went wrong, when it went wrong, and the names of employees who helped you or did not help you. You may need this information if you write a letter to the manager of the hotel to complain about the service.

5. *Walk away.*

If you are not getting any response about getting a good rate, you might mention what the rate is next door or on a similar property. If you use this technique, be prepared to walk or to keep the regular rate if the rate is not reduced. If you had a bad experience at the hotel, and you want to lodge a complaint, write directly to the manager of the hotel, since he has the authority to offer you something. Be sure you have all the facts and times and names of those involved. On the way home, jot down everything you can remember about the problem. When you write this letter, you may want to say how upsetting it was for you. Keeping your cool is not as important with a hotel as it might be with your boss or spouse. Be sure to state what you want. Do you want a certificate for a free room or just an apology? If you do not get an answer from the hotel manager, then send copies of the letter to the customer service department and/or to the president of the company. I have found that sending a letter to the president can have good results. I have gotten responses from someone else when they see that the letter has gone to the president.

B. How to Negotiate with a Doctor

Many of us are intimidated when going to the doctor. When we feel sick and anxious, we may be reluctant to question the doctor. Here are some suggestions for being prepared when going to the doctor so you can negotiate like a pro.

1. *Don't assume that anyone knows more about your medical situation than you do.*

Don't assume that a doctor, especially a new doctor, has read your file. It is up to you to tell your doctor any special medical issues in your past. If there is some follow-up that was suggested at the last appointment and is not mentioned, bring it up yourself. If you have not been to the doctor for a while, she is not going to remember the details of your history. She is going to rely on the notes in her file, and they might be fairly cryptic. She has hundreds of patients, and you have only yourself. As mentioned above, many patients are intimidated by their doctors and are afraid to question or get clarification. This is not a time to worry about being polite or nosey. It is very important that you understand everything the doctor says. If you have any questions, do not hesitate to ask her. If you don't understand the answer, ask again. This is why I suggest that you bring a friend or relative to any important meeting with your doctor. This is particularly important if you have been sedated. Your friend can take notes for you.

2. *Keep track of the paperwork.*
It is your responsibility to have a copy of all your records in your own file. This will come in handy when you are giving your medical history to a new doctor or for a new procedure. Have the telephone numbers and faxes of all your doctors. Even though I went to another doctor in the same medical complex, I was asked for the telephone numbers for my other doctors. I take a copy of a business card for every doctor I visit and then staple all the business cards to the cover of my folder so this information is readily available. Just because one of your doctors is in the same hospital, don't assume the records are readily available. A friend of mine had a CAT (computerized axial tomography) scan done in an office of a medical complex of a hospital, but the record was not available in the hospital's database. Ask for your own CD or copy of any test. Instead of relying on the hospital's or doctor's records, you can just bring your own CD to your appointment. Be sure to ask for it back. In addition, you can ask for a copy of any report. If the report is faxed or e-mailed to your doctor, ask them to email it to you as well. Many medical complexes use software to maintain the patient's access to their records. My doctor uses a program called My Chart which is used nationwide. If access to your medical record is available, be sure to register online so you can get the benefits of accessing your records, your test results and processing your drug prescriptions

3. *Bring a friend to any procedure or appointment, especially if sedated.*
Four ears are always better than two. If you have been sedated, you may be a little shaky. It may be hard to remember what was said by the doctor or nurse. You can assign your friend or relative the job of writing everything down so you can read it when you are more stabilized later on. Even if you have not been sedated, it still might be a good idea to bring someone to listen to the doctor. When a patient gets a diagnosis of a serious disease, it is really hard to concentrate. Another person can ask the doctor some questions as to the next steps and can also give you moral support.

4. *Don't be afraid to ask for a prescription*
If you are having a procedure that may cause anxiety or claustrophobia such as an MRI (magnetic resonance imaging), ask for anxiety medication.

Sometimes the doctor forgets about this. Of course, if you do take some medication, you will need someone to drive you home. This works out because your friend can then take notes after the procedure is over as indicated above.

5. *Don't be afraid to ask for a second opinion.*
Don't be afraid or feel guilty that asking for a second opinion might hurt your doctor's feelings. You are not being disloyal. It is your right to get a second opinion. You can even ask your doctor for a referral. This is your life, and it is prudent in many circumstances to see what a second and sometimes a third doctor says. Be sure to check your insurance in advance to see what is covered.

6. *Do your research. Know your insurance.*
You need to know what is covered by your health insurance. You may be able to save money just by reviewing your EOB (explanation of benefits,) especially if you have had a hospital stay. The EOB is just an explanation of what is covered by the insurance; it is not a bill for services. Don't pay anything until you get the actual bill. However, reviewing the EOB right away for errors can save you money and effort later on. It is helpful if you understand your insurance policy. Be vigilant if your doctor or a hospital wants money up front. For example, if you have not met your deductible, your doctor may request payment up front. If you have already met your deductible, have them call the insurance company itself to double-check.

The customer service reps are reading a screen that explains the details of your insurance program. It is easy for one of those reps to misread or make an assumption based on what he remembers about the policy. A doctor's office may do the same thing. It may think you are supposed to pay a co-pay when, in fact, you do not. Know the difference between a diagnostic test and a non-diagnostic test. That may determine whether you are covered. If you are on Medicare, be sure to let your doctor or hospital know whether it is primary or secondary. If you are still working, Medicare is generally secondary to your private insurance. If you are retired, then Medicare is going to be primary.

7. *Can you negotiate fees?*
When we think of Norman Rockwell posters of the family doctor, we think of patients paying their bills with chickens or eggs. Those days are over, but is it possible to negotiate doctors' fees? If you have insurance, your insurance company has already negotiated reduced rates for your group, and it would

be unlikely that you can negotiate lower rates. In fact, the doctor is probably prohibited from doing that according to his agreement with the provider.

However, if you do not have insurance or want a procedure that is not covered by insurance such as voluntary cosmetic surgery or dental work, you may want to give it a try. For example, your doctor may offer some kind of installment plan or want you to put the charges on a credit card. Offer to pay cash and see if you can get a discount. If you have two children who need orthodontia, see if the doctor will give you a discount for the second child.

C. How to Negotiate with a Car Dealer

Here are some tips to use when purchasing a vehicle. I used these techniques when I bought my last car.

1. *Be prepared and do your research.*
Being prepared is very important when buying a car. Before even going to the showroom, one should first look at the ads in the newspaper and look at car sales at Edmunds.com or a similar website. That will give you an idea what is available and the going prices. In my situation, we actually went to a lot after it was closed and looked at the cars that we liked and saw the prices. One car model had a special discount of $7,000. There was also a special for zero percent financing. The next day we called and asked the receptionist about the $7,000 discount. She told us that the $7,000 discount did not apply when using the zero percent financing However, she did tell us there was a $3,000 discount when using the zero percent discount. That was useful information because we now knew that the $3,000 discount was a given, so in order to save any money, we would have to negotiate a higher discount. Don't go to the showroom until you have done your research and are fully prepared. You need to know what you want to buy before you get there.

2. *Bring a friend and give him or her a role.*
Buying a car should be a group effort. Bring a friend or relative or two. In my case, I brought my son and very pregnant daughter-in-law. We each had a role so that whatever was said, my daughter-in-law's role was to say, "Let's go home and think it over." My son was the voice of reason. We knew that sometimes the dealer's deal is so tempting that we would be inclined to accept it on the spot. We agreed that no matter how enticing the deal was, I would

ask to speak in private with my family to discuss the details. This kind of negotiation is very stressful, and it is nice to have friends or family at your side for moral support.

3. *Read the fine print and know all the costs.*
Our strategy was to have a dollar amount limit. I did not want to pay over $25,000 for the car no matter what. We met with the sales rep, but it was hard to follow what he was saying. It sounded as though he was speaking gibberish about the various costs. At that point, we brought out our checklist, and we wrote down all the costs discussed and added them up ourselves. Then we educated ourselves on these individual costs. We also decided which extras we wanted.

Look carefully at the sticker price to see where the extra or hidden fees are. Try to determine if there is any leeway. Since our strategy was not to pay more than $25,000, it really did not matter where the discounts came from. A deal breaker was anything over $25,000. As it turned out, this was the last day of the month, which turns out to be an excellent time to buy a car because the regional dealerships are competitive as to who has the most sales each month. Therefore, the dealers may be willing to go a little lower if they can get the sale by the end of the day.

Be careful about add-ons like extension of warranty and extra maintenance programs. When I bought my last car, I felt some pressure to add those programs and I called my rep the next day and told him that I no longer wanted those extra coverages. I wasn't really trying to negotiate at that moment. They responded by saying they would give me a good discount, which would represent "cost" to them. I decided to take that offer. Sometimes it depends on how much mileage you think you will have on the vehicle. I have a friend with the same car, but she has about 4000 miles to my 30,000 miles. My warranty would expire earlier than hers because of the high mileage.

4. *Ask for one last thing.*
I knew which car I wanted and knew that I would probably leave the showroom with that particular car. It was the color I wanted and had the special features that were on my wish list. However, I wanted to get the best financial deal possible. If the dealer says the price cannot go any lower, then see if anything else can be added to the deal as a sweetener. Is there an accessory you want

such as special floor mats or a steering wheel cover? Be creative and flexible. If there are two similar cars, perhaps you could switch to the better car for the same price you are negotiating. Maybe you can negotiate free service for the car and a free car rental if it is not already provided. Your list is only limited by your imagination.

5. *Stick to your guns, and don't say yes right away.*

As my mother used to say, "It does not hurt to ask; the worst that can happen is that he says no." If you think the dealer has made its final offer, stick to your guns and try at least one more round. In my case, the dealer came back with an offer that was $300 more than $25,000. It was so close that part of me wanted to just pay the extra $300 and sign the agreement. I forced myself to say that I wanted the sales rep to go back one more time to see if he could come down to the $25,000. The rep did came back and said he would go with the lower price, probably because it was the end of the month and it was not that much more money. If the dealer had stuck with the price, I probably would have paid it, but the dealer did not know that and probably did not want to risk losing the sale.

D. How to Negotiate with a Phone Company or Other Utility

Have you ever opened your phone bill and found the amount is double or triple the amount of your last bill? Here are some tips on negotiating with your phone company and negotiating like a pro.

1. *Call the phone company immediately.*

I had a phone bill that was twice the previous month's bill. I did not have the time to call the phone company right away. I thought it might be a one-time irregularity and would wait and see what the next month's bill looked like. That was a big mistake. The error did not go away and was compounded the next month. When I did call, the phone company saw the problem right away. I had been using up my rollover minutes, and now I was way over the amount of minutes on my plan. The moral of this story is that you should call right away so you can cut your losses because the problem is not going to go away by itself. If I had called when I first saw the problem, I could have saved myself some aggravation and some money as well. Don't think the problem is going to go away without some intervention on your part.

2. Ask the phone company how the problem can be resolved.

Ask the phone company how this situation can be resolved so it does not happen again. Ask what all the options are, and what is required in each one. Ask them if there are any other alternatives. Sometimes the rep is so used to up-selling you into the next higher plan that you are not really getting all the facts. The rep might tell you something if you ask for the specific information, but she might not voluntarily give you that information without some prompting. In my situation I needed a plan with more minutes. My base monthly charge would now be a little higher but nowhere near the phone bill I had just gotten.

3. Ask the phone company to "rerate" your past bill.

I asked if my bill could be reviewed and adjustments made for the previous bills. I found out that this review and adjustment is called "rerating." That means that the phone company will calculate my current bill using the requirements of the "new plan," and, in this case, I got a credit for the difference. I also asked the rep to rerate the previous month, and I got a credit for that as well. The rep was reluctant at first to rerate the second month's bill, and another rep might have refused, saying that I should have called earlier. If you don't ask for something, the phone company usually won't suggest it. That is why my first tip is to call the phone company as soon as possible.

Don't pay your bill until the credit has taken effect. You can usually get an extension on the payment date because of the changes in the plan. This way you don't have to pay the original bill because the credit will offset it. You can check your balance, and when you have gotten the credit, you can pay the rest of the bill.

4. Do any changes to your plan affect your contract date?

I found out that my new plan with the additional minutes had an impact on the "mobile to mobile" plan that I was already on. I was on a special promotion, and in order to keep it, I was told I would have to sign a new contract for an additional eleven months. I decided that I did not want to add that much time to my contract and dropped that plan so I would not have to sign a new contract. When my contract was up, I decided to switch companies altogether. You should specifically ask if any change you make to your plan results in an extension of your contract's expiration date. You can tell the phone company that you will change companies as soon as you can to see if that makes a difference. Lately I have seen promotions encouraging phone users to change companies and the phone company offering to pay the fees to do so.

E. How to Negotiate Buying Art and Collectibles

I love the stories in the newspaper about a person or couple with limited means, such as a janitor or librarian, who was able to amass an extensive collection of art and then bequeathed the collection to a museum or a college. Often the bequest comes as a complete surprise, and everyone wonders how a person with limited finances was able to accumulate such a collection. Here are some tips for negotiating when collecting art.

1. *Discover new artists and talent.*

Serious collectors usually have a lifelong obsession with collecting. Looking for their next piece is both fun and adventurous. They look for new ideas in art and try to buy artists' works before they become famous. I recently visited the Dali Museum in St. Petersburg, Florida, which has the largest collection of Dali paintings in the United States. A. Reynolds Morse, the donor to the museum, became friends with Salvador Dali from the 1940s to the 1980s and was able to purchase many of his art pieces. Of course, we all can't get in on the ground floor and become an early patron of a soon-to-be famous artist. However, one can become knowledgeable and try to "discover" new talent before an artist is well-known, and the prices are much higher.

2. *Do your research, and go where the art is.*

Art is everywhere. Get to know what is available in your area and go to art events wherever they are. That may be world-class museums, well-known galleries, artist openings, or more impromptu events in unknown neighborhoods or on street corners. These collectors follow their artists' careers for decades. They collect many works of the same artists so they understand the artists and their various stages and phases. Any books written on your artist or collections can be an invaluable tool for your collecting. That can help you discover what is common and what is rare. Over the years I have had collections of vintage lithograph sand pails, Planters Peanuts (Mr. Peanuts) collectibles, 1950s lunch boxes, Holt Howard 1950s pixie collectibles and glass banks. Books have been written for each of these collectibles, and I have found them very useful. Many of these avid collectors have a club and/

or newsletter with annual meetings to discuss, swap, and sell pieces in their collections. These are very serious collectors whose passion is an adventure, and a lot of fun.

3. *Get a reality check. What is it really worth?*

eBay and other online websites are invaluable tools for collectors, especially if they want to collect from the comfort of their home. It makes the thrill of the hunt much more accessible to many more people. However, in my opinion, nothing beats seeing something tucked away in a corner of an old antique store that is exactly what you are looking for. You can use eBay sales as an indicator in tandem with your book or books on the subject. Depending on the rarity, some of the prices in your book may be higher or lower depending on the market right now. For example, when beanie babies were popular in the '90s, some particular beanies sold for hundreds of dollars. If you have an old guide, you will be misinformed if you try to use it today. Most beanie babies are worthless today. With the ailing economy, many of these collectibles, except for the rarest, are probably not worth as much in the market. When you are checking eBay listings, be sure to only look at the sales. An item may have a listing price of $500, but if it does not sell at that price and the average price for others on eBay is $100, you could be misled.

4. *When opportunity knocks, answer the door.*

I used to work in Winter Park, Florida, where the Charles Hosmer Morse Museum houses the most comprehensive Louis Comfort Tiffany collection in the world, including jewelry, pottery, art glass, leaded-glass windows and lamps, and the Tiffany-designed chapel interior for the 1893 World's Columbian Exposition in Chicago.

The museum also contains leaded glass from Laurelton Hall, Tiffany's gorgeous home on Long Island, which was built between 1902 and 1905. Laurelton Hall was destroyed by fire in 1957 after Tiffany's death. Tiffany's daughter called Jeannette and Hugh McKean, founders of the museum (Hugh was also president of Rollins College and Jeannette was on the Board of Trustees,) and asked if they wanted to salvage what was left after the fire. This was quite a "fire sale," and they bought everything that was salvageable at a reasonable price. Many years later, in 2010, a wing of the Morse Museum opened that now exhibits much of the glass salvaged from Laurelton Hall. As they say, opportunity only knocks once and often it does not come at an opportune time. If you get an opportunity, do everything you can within reason and without bankrupting yourself to take that opportunity.

5. *Always haggle about the price*

If opportunity has knocked, and you really want a piece of art, be creative if you feel that you cannot pay the asking price. You can start by asking if that is the best price. Usually at an art fair or a gallery, there is some leeway on the price. If you like two paintings, see if you can get a discount by buying more than one. Sometimes you can get an early draft rather than the original painting or drawing. Ask for layaway or a payment plan. I saw a woman on the *Antiques Road Show* who said that when her husband asked her what she wanted for Christmas, she said he could pay off her debt to an art dealer. She said this was her best Christmas present ever.

Always come to the artist with cash rather than a check, if possible. Starving artists always appreciate cash, and the next time you might even get a discount because you are now friends. If you don't see something you like, ask what is in the back or in the warehouse. Your next piece may be hidden somewhere. Artists generally need money, but you can still try to barter with your skills. You could offer to babysit or dog sit. If you are a licensed massage therapist, maybe you could pay with some money and add a massage or two. Commission a project and give a down payment now and pay when it is completed. This will give you some time to get the money for your commission.

Chapter 12

How to Negotiate on eBay

1. What is eBay and how does it work?

eBay (see glossary) is an online auction for buyers and sellers. It uses an automatic bidding system to make bidding on auctions more convenient and less time-consuming. When you make a bid, you enter the maximum amount you'd be willing to pay. This information is kept confidential and is not divulged to buyers or sellers. The eBay system compares your bids to any other bids on the item and, in effect, the system places bids on your behalf. It uses only as much of your bid as is needed to be the highest bidder. If another bidder has bid a higher amount, then you will be outbid, and you have the opportunity to make a higher bid.

Here is an example of how it works. You see a Fender guitar that you want to buy. The maximum you are willing to bid is $300. The minimum bid is $50. If someone else has already secretly bid over $300, then you will get a message that you have been outbid. If the highest bid before you bid was $200, your only bid will be shown at the next increment, or $205. If no one else bids, then you will get the item for the $205, not the $300.

eBay has revolutionized how people buy and sell antiques, collectibles, and new items. eBay does not handle the item; it only provides the online framework to bid and charges insertion fees and a percentage commission of the final bid. You could buy a $1 poster or a $100,000 car, but the concepts are basically the same regardless of the value of the item.

2. Look at the listing

As an eBay buyer, you should read the whole listing and make sure that you have not missed any pertinent information such as a handling charge or price of shipping outside the United States When a buyer buys two or more items from the same buyer, he usually expects the seller to allow him to combine shipping and save on postage by only shipping one package. If that is not the case, the listing should say so. Some sellers are a little sneaky and bury some of the details of the listing in the small print. You need to look for words like "refurbished," "like new," or "slightly used." The seller's idea of "like new" could be a lot different from the buyer's idea of "like new." If you do not read the listing carefully, which is in effect his offer to you, then you cannot complain afterward. You have to live with what was in the listing. If you do have questions for the seller about the condition of the item, combining shipping costs, or picking up the item, then those issues should be addressed to the seller before the auction ends.

3. Know what the item is worth.

This is particularly important when bidding on eBay. You can see the final prices of other items that have sold on eBay. This is an invaluable tool to determine how high to bid. Be sure you are checking a comparable item. If you are looking at a coin that is circulated, it is not going to be worth the same as a proof coin. Be sure you are not comparing apples and oranges, but apples and apples. Also, look at the condition of the item. If there are flaws such as cracks, dings, or crazing, that can affect the value. Factor in the value of repairs and flaws when bidding. Don't bid as though it was perfect. As a seller, you can get a reality check by looking at other eBay values.

You may think you have a rare and unusual item, and a buyer would be willing to pay a premium for it in an antique shop. However, now that eBay is an international source of goods, there may be many items similar to yours for sale, and that can deflate the price. It is a simple case of supply and demand. However, special qualities about your item such as a low mintage, a rare date, or a rare mint, such as Carson City, may give your item special value over the other coins. If your item is one of a kind or is in pristine condition, buyers may be willing to pay a premium price because they know it might be a long time, if ever, before another item like it will be sold on eBay.

4. Be willing to apologize.

Being willing to apologize is particularly important in eBay transactions. When things go wrong, it is best to show some empathy and apologize for the inconvenience or miscommunication even if you believe it is the post office's fault for losing the package or the package arriving broken. For some people, it is hard to accept blame or responsibility when they know in their hearts that they did nothing wrong. If you are this kind of person, just keep in mind that you are trying to have a good transaction, and you need to be willing to compromise in order to reach that goal. Try to put yourself into the buyer's shoes. He paid promptly for the item, and it is not his fault either. The eBay Feedback system is an incentive for sellers to give good customer service.

5. Does the other side want something other than money?

What can you do to make the buyer happy? The buyer may want his money back or an apology. If the item is broken, you might arrange for someone to come to the buyer's home to repair it. This is particularly helpful in computer sales. You can always find a computer tech at the buyer's location. Usually the other side will be unwilling to take the time or spend the money to send an item back and then wait for you to determine what repairs are needed and then wait for its return. If you are out of the ordered item, perhaps you can offer the buyer a better one in stock. Explain what the differences are so the buyer will know he is getting a better deal. The other side may balk if you insist that he pay any additional shipping. You may want to offer free shipping. Sometimes the other side just wants an explanation of what happened. If the item took three weeks to get to the buyer's house, what was the explanation? Was it the seller's fault or someone else's?

6. Don't make promises you cannot keep.

If you know the shipping is going to be delayed, tell the buyer. Some buyers stay at home all day waiting for delivery, and when no delivery occurs, they are furious. Always give yourself some leeway when making promises. It is better for the buyer to be pleasantly surprised that the item arrived a day before you predicted rather than the other way around. If you know any item is out of stock, be realistic about the true delivery date. If you say you will help the buyer out, don't change your mind when you find out the true cost or the time involved. If you cannot keep your promise, then don't make it in the first place.

7. Everyone makes mistakes.

No one is perfect, and everyone makes mistakes. When you buy and sell on eBay, it is inevitable that there will be mistakes. It is just human nature. The seller will send item A to person B and item B to person A. After a package has been mailed, the seller finds the belt at home for the dress just shipped. The best approach is to acknowledge that a mistake has been made and figure out how to undo the mistake and get on with your life instead of saying something like, "You were careless," or "You should have packed better." This way you skip the recriminations and go straight to a solution. If you are the one making the mistake, you should sincerely apologize and see how you can make it up to the other party.

8. Followup after the winning bid.

As an eBay seller, you need to communicate regularly with your buyers to keep them informed. They need to know how much money they owe, including postage and handling. They should be informed when payment is received and told when to expect the delivery and the method of shipping. Tracking is indispensable and worth the expense. Both sides can check the tracking and will know if a delay occurred and if it is the carrier's fault. If the item is lost, and you do not have tracking, no one will know for sure what happened to the item. Keeping the buyer informed is good customer service, and the buyer feels that he is being treated in a respectful way.

9. What is feedback?

Each time you buy or sell something on eBay, you have an opportunity to leave feedback about your experience. Feedback is a way to evaluate a member's reputation and is the backbone of the eBay process. Feedback consists of a positive, negative, or neutral rating along with a short comment. Since Feedback becomes a permanent part of their record, buyers are encouraged to contact sellers to try to resolve any issues before leaving neutral or negative Feedback. Buyers can revise Feedback they've left for sellers in the case of a mistake.

Along with an overall rating, buyers can also rate sellers on specific aspects of the transaction with *detailed seller ratings,* which are anonymous and don't count toward the overall Feedback Scores. The buyer can rate on a 1-5 scale on the following topics:

    A. How accurate was the item description?

    B. How satisfied were you with the seller's communication?

    C. How quickly did the seller ship the item?

    D. How reasonable were the shipping and handling charges?

10. eBay Sellers' Feedback Issues

Sellers build their reputation based on their feedback ratings from buyers. Sellers can leave only positive ratings or no ratings for buyers so that buyers feel free to leave honest Feedback without fear of retaliation. Since sellers are not able to leave negative or neutral Feedback for buyers, sellers need other tools and safeguards in place to protect them against unfair negative or neutral Feedback.

Here are some ways sellers and eBay are working together to protect sellers' reputations and promote a fair marketplace:

A. *Sellers can add buyer requirements to their listings to prevent unwanted bidders.*

Sellers can block buyers with too many policy violations, unpaid items, or buyers who are not registered with PayPal.

B. *Sellers can require buyers to pay right away.*

If sellers use **Buy it Now**, they can require buyers to pay immediately using PayPal.

C. *Sellers have an easy way to report problems with buyers.*

Sellers can use the *seller reporting hub* to report an unpaid item, Feedback extortion, or any other problem with a buyer. eBay investigates all reports and will remove any negative or neutral Feedback in violation of eBay policy.

D. *eBay provides enhanced Feedback protection for unpaid items.*

eBay will also remove negative or neutral Feedback when it is clear that the buyer did not intend to complete the transaction. An example of this is when the buyer buys the item elsewhere or has a family emergency.

E. *eBay proactively looks for Feedback abuses and takes action against it.*

eBay investigates buyers who leave positive Feedback but low Detailed Seller Ratings.

F. *eBay removes Feedback from suspended buyers.*

eBay removes all neutral or negative Feedback left by suspended buyers so it won't negatively affect sellers' reputations.

G. *eBay educates buyers.*

If there are problems with a purchase, eBay will ask the buyer to contact the seller directly to try to work things out before leaving negative or neutral Feedback.

11. How can buyers' negative feedback be revised?

A seller may ask a buyer to revise negative or neutral Feedback that the buyer gave. When this happens, the seller will receive an email notification from eBay. If the buyer agrees to revise the seller's Feedback, he will click the **Accept Request** button to display the Revise Seller's Feedback page. Then the buyer will select the button that indicates the revised Feedback rating. Note that the buyer cannot change a neutral rating to a negative rating. The buyer will enter a revised comment in the Revise Comment text box. The buyer will select the number of stars for the revised rating for each of the areas in the rating. Then the buyer will click the **Revise Feedback** button. After reviewing the revised Feedback, the buyer will confirm the changed Feedback.

If the buyer decides to decline the seller's request to revise Feedback, the buyer will click the **Decline request** button and the buyer will click the **Keep original Feedback** button. Then the buyer will select the button that best describes the reasons that he is declining the seller's request. Then the buyer will submit the button.

There are some situations when the sellers can initiate changes to feedback or comments if the buyer agrees. If a buyer wants to change the negative or neutral feedback she left for a seller, she cannot do this unilaterally. However, the buyer can advise the seller to request the change. Here are some situations where the buyer can revise the feedback comment, rating or detailed seller ratings. If the seller fixes a problem with the transaction or if the buyer accidentally left the wrong feedback, the seller can request a feedback revision. However, eBay does limit the feedback revisions for sellers fixing the problem to five feedback revisions for every one thousand feedbacks so that sellers can focus on providing great customer service in the first place and not fixing problems only when they happen.

12. eBay will remove or change feedback ratings or comments if:

A. Feedback contains inappropriate comments or violates a feedback policy.

B. Feedback contains personally identifiable information about another member, such as member's address, phone number or email.

C. Feedback not related to a sale, including a comment, reply or follow-up related to a different sale.

D. Feedback contains political, religious, social or other commentary, rather than comments about the sale.

E. Feedback contains language that is profane, vulgar, obscene, or racist, as well as comments that contain adult material or physical threats.

F. Negative feedback comments that directly contradict a positive rating when the comment is posted by the *seller*. This type of contradictory comment left by a *buyer* is not removable.

G. Feedback contains links or promotional language which encourages buyers to purchase outside of eBay.

H. Feedback includes references to law enforcement investigations or eBay or PayPal investigations.

I. Feedback can be removed if a buyer or seller violated the eBay extortion policy.

J. However, Feedback comments containing comments such as "fraud," "liar," "cheater," "scam artist" or "con man" are strongly discouraged, but they will not be removed.

13. eBay Buyer Protection Plan
A. Buyers are eligible for Buyer Protection Plan if they

1. Made the purchase on eBay.

2. Paid using the eBay checkout process with an approved payment method like PayPal, Bill Me Later, or direct credit card purchase.

3. Made a purchase that is not specifically excluded from protection, like real estate.

4. Made the purchase within the 45 days preceding the claim.

5. Have a good faith dispute with the seller.

B. eBay will intervene when the seller has failed to adequately resolve the dispute. Buyers that file a successful claim under the program are usually:

1. Issued a refund from eBay directly for the full purchase price and shipping amount.
2. Required to return the unsatisfactory item to the seller.
3. Absolved of any further connection with the transaction or obligation to the seller.

14. eBay Vehicle Purchase Protection Plan (VPP) covers certain vehicle transactions up to $10,000.

A. VPP is automatically included at no additional cost when you complete the purchase of an eligible vehicle on eBay. The types of fraud include:

1. Non-delivery of the vehicle.
2. Undisclosed defects in the vehicle's title.
3. Certain undisclosed defects with the vehicle.

B. eBay provides these warning signs for vehicles or any other kind of transaction:

1. Vehicles advertised well below what it is worth may be tempting but should be a red flag. If it appears to be too good to be true, it probably is.
2. You are unable to see the vehicle in person first or have it physically inspected prior to payment.
3. There is an urgency to complete the sale quickly because the seller has a health or family issue, is being deployed to the military, moving out of state/country or is going through divorce/marriage.
4. Seller pushes to get money in advance and transferred through a fast payment method, or sent to a fake escrow account to avoid you as the buyer losing out on the deal before another buyer purchases the item first.
5. You found the vehicle on another website and the seller tells you eBay will protect the transaction.
6. Private seller offers free shipping of the vehicle to you. Criminals may tell you they have access to transportation resources possibly through

their employer or because they are in the military and can coordinate the delivery for you.

15. Suspicious emails, phishing and spoofing.

Criminals want to lure you into feeling safe and may also disguise their websites or emails to look as though they are from eBay, when they are not. Here are warning signs:

1. Emails have poor grammar, misspelled words, or incorrect punctuation.
2. Emails may be overly formal or sound very mechanical and include general terms like Good Day or Dear Sir.
3. Emails are not sent from the eBay.com domain. Criminals may have a recognizable word in their email name such as eBay or VPP but they are not sent by eBay.
4. Email contains false information like invoice numbers, transaction case IDs or VPP case IDs.
5. If you are suspicious about an email that claims to be from eBay, first sign in and see if you have the same message in your message tab. If you do not see it, the message is probably fake and you should forward it to Spoof@ebay.com.
6. Do not give anyone your account information for PayPal, eBay, or a credit card in response to an email that requests information.
7. It might look like an official e-mail from eBay or PayPal, but a scam artist is trying to get your account information and steal your identity so he can use your account and positive feedback to sell items on eBay or get funds from your PayPal account.
8. Don't even open these e-mails, but if you do, do not put in your account information. If you make a mistake and think that you may have been spoofed by one of these scams, contact eBay, PayPal, or your credit company immediately so they can close down your account before the account information is used.
9. If you receive such an email, forward it to spoof@ebay.com or spoof@paypal.com or to your bank.
10. eBay has taken precautions so that all messages to eBay members are sent through their My eBay site for each eBay user
11. If you still have questions as to whether the vehicle or other item being offered is legitimate, contact eBay Customer Service.

16. eBay Resolution Center

The eBay Resolution Center recommends that its members communicate with each other. If there is a problem with a transaction, you can start the resolution process. If you paid for your eBay item with PayPal, you can report your problem on either eBay or PayPal. If you file a claim with PayPal while an eBay claim is open, your eBay claim will be closed and PayPal will proceed with your case. You can file with PayPal after the conclusion of any eBay claim (if within the 180 day time frame) if you are not satisfied with the outcome of your eBay claim. The first step is to contact the other member by opening a request through the Resolution Center. The second step is to use the tools at the Resolution Center. The Seller has three business days to respond. If the seller does not respond satisfactorily, the case is escalated and sent to eBay for review.

17. Credit card company.

If eBay can't help you, your credit card company may be able to assist you. Many credit card companies provide some level of purchase protection, so contact your credit card company to learn more about its programs. If you are covered, this is a good reason to pay for eBay purchases with that credit card. If you do not receive the merchandise, you can put through a claim with your credit card company. Another good way to pay is through PayPal or one of the other services eBay recommends. PayPal sends funds from a verified bank account or credit card directly to the seller online. Sellers who choose to send to a non-verified address will not be protected by PayPal's buyer protection system.

For more info, visit eBay's Customer Support Page or the PayPal Resolution Center.

Chapter 13 | WHAT'S NEXT WHEN NEGOTIATIONS FAIL?

A certain number of negotiations will reach an impasse, and that deadlock cannot be broken by the parties. You will need to make a decision as to whether you want to go to another forum, such as mediation or arbitration or drop the case altogether,

A. Should you go to mediation?

If you have made some progress but don't like dealing with each other, it might be a good time to bring in a mediator, who can work with the parties in individual caucuses. The mediator will facilitate, and the parties do not have to work directly with each other anymore. You may want to read my second book in this series, *How to Mediate Like a Pro: 42 Rules for Mediating Disputes,* which has won twelve book awards and is based on my experience as a mediator.

Mediation is a process in which parties use a neutral facilitator, the mediator, to help the parties resolve their dispute. The parties do not deal with each other directly; all communication goes through the mediator. Although the mediator will meet with both parties together, much of the work gets done in the caucus (see glossary, Appendix A) when the mediator meets with one party alone. The caucus allows the parties to discuss the merits of the case with the mediator without the other party present. The parties can also tell the mediator in caucus what information to divulge, when to divulge it, and what not to divulge. The caucus also allows the mediator to be the devil's advocate (see glossary) and to discuss the strengths and weaknesses of the dispute.

The mediator does not make a decision like a judge or arbitrator. The mediator facilitates what the parties want. Sometimes the parties have already tried to negotiate directly with the other party, but the negotiations reached an impasse or deadlock. When there is animosity between the parties, mediation can be successful because the mediator acts as a buffer between the parties.

B. Should you go to arbitration?

If mediation does not work, you may want to consider arbitration. The arbitrator will make a decision based on the facts and evidence presented to her at a hearing. In mediation, the parties resolve the case themselves with the help of the mediator. The parties need to look at how much they are willing to spend and how important the final resolution is to them before deciding how to proceed.

In arbitration the parties present their arguments in a hearing format to an arbitrator who makes the decision. The parties may have already tried to resolve it themselves through negotiation or mediation. By going to arbitration, they have given the decision-making power to the arbitrator, who acts as a judge. The arbitration hearing is much more informal than court. Arbitration can either be binding or non-binding. Labor arbitration is binding, which means that the decision cannot be appealed or overturned by a court unless the arbitrator showed bias or discrimination in the decision. The courts have long recognized that labor arbitrators have a specialized knowledge of labor law that judges generally do not have. An arbitration that is not binding means that the parties can reject the decision. The parties may not take a non-binding arbitration seriously if they have the power to reject the decision. It is more like a dress rehearsal to flush out the issues.

Alternate dispute resolution (known as ADR) is an alternative to taking a case to court. Collectively, procedures such as negotiation, mediation, arbitration, mediation-arbitration (med-arb), and arbitration-mediation (arb-med) are a cheaper and faster alternative to litigation. In addition, the parties have more control of the outcome of the case, especially in negotiation or mediation. If the parties must work with each other after the hearing, such as the parents in child custody or visitation cases, ADR is preferable over going to court. The animosity between the parents may be increased as a result of an adversarial process.

C. Should you go to mediation-arbitration or arbitration-mediation?

A. Mediation-arbitration, known as med-arb, is a hybrid process. An arbitrator is chosen, but if both parties agree, he will mediate the case first, and then if that does not succeed, he will arbitrate the case and make a decision. The advantage is that you can have two processes done by the same person. The disadvantage is that the arbitrator may learn things about the case in the mediation phase that might affect the arbitration decision.

B. Arbitration-mediation, known as arb-med, is a hybrid process where the arbitration takes place first, and both parties present their cases. The arbitrator writes an arbitration decision but does not show it to the parties. Then the arbitrator becomes the mediator, and he conducts the mediation. If the mediation is resolved, then the written opinion is not revealed. If the mediation is not resolved, the arbitrator's written opinion is revealed. The advantage of doing the arbitration first is that the arbitrator is not influenced by information he may receive later in confidential caucus. The disadvantage is that the arbitrator may have conducted an arbitration that was not necessary.

Chapter 14

How to Negotiate Anything, Anytime, Anywhere

10 Questions to get a better deal

When I give talks about my books, participants often ask me what questions to ask to get the best deal. As a result of those comments, I started compiling a list of questions that will help negotiators get the best deal possible. You can use these questions on everyday issues like buying at thrift markets and getting your lawn mowed.

1. What is the best you can do?

Usually what I call "wiggle room" is built into any price of an item or service. It is human nature for the seller to inflate a price. If the seller gets that price, fine. We all know someone who does not like to haggle and will pay the asking price if she has the money and wants the item. Other buyers love a bargain and will never pay full price. It can be embarrassing for some, but really it does not hurt to ask for a discount, even in places where you don't think you can get one. The worst that can happen is that the seller says no.

2. Is this the lowest price?

This sounds like the same question, but it is a little different. If the first question does not work, try this one to see if you can get a response. Asking the question a different way may get the seller's attention. My advice to sellers when someone shows some interest in an item is to try to work with them. That person may end up being the only person remotely interested in the item. Again, if you get a negative answer, you can move on or pay the ticket price.

3. What is the lowest price if I buy two or three or ten items?

Try buying in bulk. Usually you can get some kind of a discount. This is a real win/win. The seller is able to sell several or all of his items. It is a lot easier to sell to one person rather than having to deal with several buyers.

4. What if I pick up the item?

You see an item, and delivery is free. However, you have a truck with you, and it is really easier to put the item in your truck rather than waiting for delivery. The seller does not have to pay someone to deliver the item, so this should be worth a nice discount.

5. Can you give me a discount because this item is chipped, a sample, or a floor model?

Often samples or floor models are on sale after a certain period of time. However, if you find some obvious defect, such as a nick or chip, this item is going to be even harder to sell. If you are willing to take a damaged item, make sure you get a good discount. Sometimes even "new" items will be chipped or scratched. Point out these defects, and see if you can get a discount. Always inspect an item before leaving the store. It is always harder to bring something back that is defective, because there may be some question as to where the damage occurred.

6. Since you are already in the neighborhood, can you mow my lawn too?

Seize the opportunity if you see a worker that you need doing a similar job in the neighborhood. The proximity, not to mention the savings on gas, may allow the worker to give you a nice discount. Time is money if he is already there. You could do this for lawn care, snow shoveling, mulching, tree trimming, or pesticide application.

7. Are you willing to do a trade or barter?

If you are a massage therapist, carpenter, or music teacher, try to trade or barter your services. I don't have any of those talents, but sometimes I will throw in a book or two to sweeten the deal.

8. Is there going to be a sale soon?

I have bought things at full price only to find out they were on sale the next day. Always ask if the item will be on sale anytime soon. If the answer is yes, perhaps the clerk will put it away for you until the sale or even give you the sales price today.

9. Can you give me an upgrade?

If you have gotten bad service, especially with a hotel or airline, always ask for an upgrade. Some companies are really into customer service and are looking for ways to exceed the expectations of the customer. Even if you have not gotten bad service, ask anyway and see what happens. Many companies use surveys after a transaction via e-mail or phone, and the employees have an incentive to do well on these customer surveys.

10. Can you throw a sweetener into the deal?

If you are getting a sofa, ask the store to throw in some pillows. If you are getting an expensive necklace, ask the jeweler to throw in a free pair of earrings.

Ask these ten questions, and you will be negotiating like a pro.

Chapter 15

Conclusion: Summary of the 41 Rules

Here is a list of all 41 rules with a short summary so you can access them quickly. I like to look at the rules before any negotiation, big or small, and then plan which ones I want to emphasize in any particular negotiation.

Rule 1: Focus on the goal. Don't be distracted by your emotions.
You can't negotiate when you are angry and out of control.

Rule 2: Look forward, not back. The past is called the past for a reason.
Wallowing in the past does not resolve current disputes.

Rule 3: You don't have to be right to settle.
It should not matter who is at fault in order to resolve a dispute.

Rule 4: Know what you want and what the other side wants.
You can't start a negotiation until you know what the issues are.

Rule 5: Be prepared, and do your research.
Preparation is key so you can defend your proposals.

Rule 6: Get a reality check. What is it really worth?
The real value may be different from what you had hoped.

Rule 7: Always have a Plan B.
Be flexible. Don't put all your eggs in one basket.

Rule 8: Find out if the other side wants something other than money.
Maybe the dispute can be resolved with an apology or change in policy.

Rule 9: Only negotiate with someone with authority.
You are wasting your time if the other negotiator doesn't have the power to settle.

Rule 10: Set the tone and look the part.
You don't get a second chance to make a good first impression.

Rule 11: Request ground rules.
Ground rules prevent chaos at the negotiating table.

Rule 12: Volunteer and take control.
If you want something done right, do it yourself.

Rule 13: Agree on the issues and prioritize them.
This saves a lot of time and effort.

Rule 14: Say what you want.
Even if you know what you want, you have to articulate it properly.

Rule 15: Never take or give no for an answer.
Be persistent. Offer alternatives.

Rule 16: It doesn't hurt to ask. If you don't ask, you don't get.
The worst that can happen is that the person says no.

Rule 17: Don't give away bargaining chips without getting something in return.
This is *quid pro quo,* this for that.

Rule 18: Always ask for one more thing or be prepared to give one more thing.
Don't leave anything on the table.

Rule 19: Know the rhythm and tempo of the negotiation.
Are you dealing with a big-picture negotiator or a detail-oriented negotiator?

Rule 20: Keep track of the paperwork.
If someone is not keeping track, there will be confusion and chaos.

Rule 21: Don't gloat.
It will infuriate the other side.

Rule 22: Be alert and keep a poker face.
You don't want the other side to know what you are thinking.

Rule 23: Don't negotiate against yourself.
Don't make an offer when you already have one on the table. Wait for a counter-offer.

Rule 24: Be a devil's advocate.
This is a safe way to point out flaws in the other side's arguments.

Rule 25: Save face.
This allows a person to get out of an embarrassing situation and keep his dignity intact.

Rule 26: Watch the other side's body language.
You can understand what someone is thinking by watching his body moves.

Rule 27: Have a temper tantrum.
In negotiations, a temper tantrum is an acting job and done sparingly.

Rule 28: Walk away.
Walk away only if you mean it. It can't be a bluff.

Rule 29: Do not overreach.
Ambushing the other side will make them want to retaliate.

Rule 30: Create a diversion such as a smoke screen, decoy, or red herring.
These diversionary tactics divert attention from the main goal to something unimportant.

Rule 31: Take it or leave it.

My way or the highway. Not recommended except perhaps at the end to close the deal.

Rule 32: Everyone makes mistakes; to err is human.

Admit any mistakes; don't hide them; apologize; and move on.

Rule 33: Be willing to apologize; to forgive is divine.

A good apology is sincere; otherwise don't bother.

Rule 34: The devil is in the details.

Be sure all loose ends are tied down.

Rule 35: Trade-off or split the difference.

Ideal tactics for closing the deal especially if the amount to be split is low.

Rule 36: Step back and look at the big picture.

Looking at the big picture gives you perspective so you can decide whether to continue.

Rule 37: Know when to hold and when to fold.

Like a poker game, you need to know when to give up or when to continue.

Rule 38: Follow up after negotiations.

You need to make sure all contingencies in the contract are done throughout its term.

Rule 39. Don't expect thanks or gratitude when it is all over.

Be glad it is over and celebrate with your team.

Rule 40: You can negotiate with difficult people.

You can resolve disputes with bullies, liars and narcissists.

Rule 41. Be ethical, and don't make promises you can't keep.

Once you lose your reputation, it is difficult to get back.

When you follow these rules, you will be negotiating like a pro.

APPENDIX A
Glossary of Negotiation Terms

alternate dispute resolution. Known as ADR, includes negotiation, mediation, arbitration, and other dispute procedures that are an alternative to going to court. Generally ADR is faster and less expensive than litigation, and the parties have more control of the outcome than if they filed a court case.

alternative facts. The phrase *alternative facts* was first used by Kellyanne Conway, White House Counsel to the President, during a Meet the Press interview in January 2017 with Chuck Todd. She used the term to discuss Sean Spicer's false statement about the size of the President's inauguration crowd. She said that Spicer was just giving "alternative facts," which was derided in the press. She later stated that she meant "alternative facts" to be "additional facts and alternative information." The phrase is widely used now. (see *fake news.*)

apology. An apology is when one party accepts blame and responsibility for his/her actions and shows some kind of remorse or regret.

arbitration. A process where parties present their arguments to a neutral arbitrator, and the arbitrator makes the decision. This is an alternative to litigation (going to court) and is one of the procedures known as alternate dispute resolution, or ADR. Labor/management arbitration is one of the oldest kinds of arbitration. The arbitrator is like a judge, while the parties make their own decisions in mediation and negotiation.

arbitration-mediation (arb-med). A hybrid process where the arbitration takes place first and both parties present their case. The arbitrator writes an arbitration decision but does not show it to the parties. Then the arbitrator becomes the mediator, and he conducts the mediation. If the mediation is resolved, then the written arbitration decision is not revealed. If the mediation is not resolved, then the arbitrator's written opinion is revealed. The advantage of doing the arbitration first is that the arbitrator is not influenced by information he may receive later in a confidential caucus. The disadvantage is that the arbitrator may have conducted an arbitration that was not necessary.

authority. Means that the person negotiating has the authority or power to make a decision and act on behalf of his employer or company. Even if a person has authority, it might only be authority up to a certain amount. It is better to know in the beginning what the person's authority is before the negotiations start. If someone does not have authority, then there is no point negotiating with him because he cannot approve any agreement.

bargaining chip. A concession that can be offered to the other side as an incentive to get something. Using the poker terminology makes the term a metaphor for the negotiation process. One should always keep some bargaining chips in reserve because they may be needed to close the deal.

binding arbitration. A type of arbitration where the arbitrator's decision is final and cannot be appealed by the parties unless the arbitrator committed fraud or showed bias.

Boulewareism. A *take it or leave it* approach to negotiation. The term is named after Lemuel Boulware, a vice president at General Electric in the 1950s. After much research as to what was best for the company, he opened the negotiations with his first, last, and best offer and told the electrical union to *take it or leave it.* The court later determined that this one-sided approach was not good faith bargaining because there was no give and take by the parties and no involvement by the union. (This is sometimes spelled **Boulewarism.**)

caucuses. Meetings held separately with each party to discuss how to resolve the dispute. It allows the party to talk about the dispute without the other party being present.

compulsive liar. Same as a *pathological liar.*

concession. Giving something up that the other party wants or agreeing with the other party. The term is used synonymously with bargaining chip. *You made too many concessions and don't have any bargaining chips left.*

confidentiality. Means that information concerning the negotiation is not divulged or discussed with outside parties during the negotiations. This can jeopardize the negotiation process. It is important to make confidentiality part of the ground rules for the negotiation. It is also important that all team members understand their obligations.

deadlock. Occurs when the parties reach impasse, and the parties cannot agree on anything further. The deadlock has to be broken, or the negotiation will have to close without resolution.

decoys. Used to mislead and lure an unsuspecting bird by setting out a realistic duck model so he will follow the decoy and allow hunters to shoot at him. This same tactic is used in negotiations. The purpose is to mislead the other, unsuspecting, party with a diversionary tactic, which is the decoy. This is similar to the **smoke screen** and **red herring**.

defined benefit retirement. The amount of the pension benefit is based on the number of years worked times a multiplier, such as 2 per cent, times the average of the top five years or something like that in the plan. Defined plans are often part of a collective bargaining agreement for police officers, firefighters and teachers, but are becoming less and less common.

defined benefit contribution. The employer contributes a percentage of salary and the employee contributes a percentage of salary and the employee manages the plan. These are called 401K plans in the private sector and 401 A Plans in the public sector.

devil's advocate. An approach that is a way to give a reality check to the other side and point out the flaws in its arguments. The expression used is *Let me play the devil's advocate.* By playing the devil's advocate, you are insulated from criticism because you are only pointing out these problems as if you were the devil.

discrimination. Treating a person adversely because of his or her race, religion, color, disability, gender, age, or national origin.

diversity. Acknowledges differences in culture and experiences. This can include age, ethnicity, class, gender, race, sexual orientation, religion, geographical location, income, marital status, and work experience.

ethics. Moral principles that govern a person's behavior. Some synonyms are: moral code, values, principles, ideals, value system, conscience. There is a distinction between *law* and ethics. Laws are the rules and regulations set by the government. If disobeyed, there may be punishment. Ethics are the moral values and principles that are part of a society. Laws and ethics can conflict with each other. Something may be legal but not ethical.

explanation of benefits (EOB). A statement sent by a health insurance company to a covered customer to explain what medical treatment or services were paid on his behalf. An EOB is not a bill for services.

face-saving. A way to allow someone to get out of an embarrassing situation with his or her dignity intact. Giving someone a way out is a tradition in many Asian countries. You are helping the other side not to look bad and not be humiliated.

fake news. A type of journalism that deliberately misinforms the reader about hoaxes. It is written with the only purpose of misleading the reader. This type of journalism used to be called yellow journalism but today the favored term is fake news. Some people will say a story is *fake news* if they don't like it. (see *alternative facts.)*

feedback. A system that allows eBay users to rate the buyer or seller in each eBay transaction. A buyer can leave a positive, neutral, or negative rating, and a comment to explain his or her satisfaction level. The feedback score is the sum of all of the ratings an eBay user received from individual users. The positive number is compared to the negative to give the user a percentage number as well. For example, a perfect score of all positives is 100 percent.

final offer. The last offer made in a negotiation. Don't call it a *final offer* if you have anything else to negotiate. Do not use the *final offer* at the beginning of negotiations; that would be *Boulwareism*, a *take it or leave it* approach. There should only be one *final offer*, and it should be a tool at the end of negotiations to close the deal (See *Boulewarism* and *take it or leave it.)*

good faith bargaining. Required by federal and state labor laws. It means that the parties have a duty to approach bargaining with the right attitude and are prepared to discuss issues and meet on a regular basis. It does not mean that the parties must come to an agreement, though. Good faith bargaining is the opposite of *Boulwareism* and *take it or leave it.*

ground rules. The procedural rules that are used for the negotiation process and agreed to by both parties. Here are some examples: *Only one person will speak at a time. Parties will be courteous at all times. Only the spokesperson can speak on behalf of the team.* Having ground rules helps the negotiation run more smoothly because all parties know the expectations in advance.

impasse. Occurs when the parties are deadlocked, and there does not appear to be any room for agreement. The impasse has to be broken, or the negotiation will have to close without resolution.

mediation. A process where parties use a neutral facilitator, called a mediator, to help the parties resolve their dispute. The parties do not deal with each other directly as in a negotiation. The mediator does not make a decision as an arbitrator or judge does. The parties resolve the case with the mediator's assistance. Mediation is a type of alternate dispute resolution, which is an alternative to going to court.

mediation-arbitration (med-arb). A hybrid process where the arbitrator is chosen, but if both parties agree, the arbitrator will mediate the case first, and then if that does not succeed, the arbitrator will arbitrate the case and make a decision. The advantage is that you can have two processes done by the same person. The disadvantage is that the arbitrator may learn things about the case in the mediation phase that might affect the arbitration decision.

negotiation. A process where parties resolve disputes with each other. The term is often used synonymously with collective bargaining. The essence of negotiation is that both parties agree to work with each other to resolve a problem or dispute. Negotiation is a type of alternate dispute resolution, which is an alternative to going to court.

negotiating against oneself. Occurs when you make another offer when there already is an offer on the table. You should always wait for a counteroffer, or you will be negotiating against yourself. For example, you offer $5,000, and then you offer $10,000 when the other party nodded no. You should have asked for a counteroffer instead. The other party might have countered with $7,500, so you have already lost $2,500.

non-binding arbitration. A type of arbitration where the arbitration decision is not binding on the parties. The parties can still go to court or to another arbitration. It is, in effect, an independent assessment of the case, which might help in resolving out of court.

online dispute resolution. Known as **ODR,** is a way to resolve disputes online and is the online equivalent of alternate dispute resolution. Online mediation is the most common form of ODR. Online mediation is not done in real time like face-to-face mediation. ODR uses technology, and its usage will increase and will probably be as common as regular ADR.

overreach. Get the better of someone by cunning, ambush, deception, or circumvention.

package offer. A way to put several proposals on the table to make the deal look more attractive. I will give you A and B and C, but we want D and E. This is sometimes called bundling and is more complex than a trade-off.

pathological liar. A person who lies all the time for no apparent reason and may not even know that he is lying.

phishing. A fake website where internet users are lured through lookalike e-mails supposedly from eBay, AOL, PayPal, and banks asking for confidential account information. If given, that information is used to access someone's account and steal his or her identity.

quid pro quo. Means *this for that*, literally, in Latin. In negotiations, it *means I will give you what you want if you give me what I want*. It is basically the same as a trade-off. Both parties can get what they want, and the problem is solved.

red herring. A tactic to mislead the other party and create a diversion. The origin of the term involved rubbing a red herring on hounds to protect the hunted fox. The hounds will smell the herring and won't be able to track the fox. A red herring is essentially a false clue or phony issue used to distract hounds, politicians, and negotiators. This is similar to *decoy* and *smoke screen*.

saving face. A way to allow someone to keep his dignity and not be humiliated.

smoke screen. A way to mask your true intent and create a diversion. In war, smoke is released to mask the location or movement of troops. In negotiations, it is a diversionary tactic to take attention away from the main objective and give attention to something of little or no importance. This is similar to the *decoy* and *red herring*.

spoof. An internet-based scheme to steal someone's identity. An e-mail is sent that looks like an official e-mail from eBay, a bank, PayPal or AOL, which lures the person to a fake website (phishing) with the purpose of tricking that person into giving confidential account information.

takeaway. A tactic threatening to take away something that is already part of a previous agreement The tactic creates the illusion of giving something to the other side which they already had.

take it or leave it. An approach used to give the other side a first, last, and firm offer and tell them you are not going to negotiate with them any longer. This is a risky approach, especially at the beginning of negotiations. It should only be used at the end of negotiations to close the deal. (See *final offer* and *Boulwareism*.)

tentative agreement. Known as a TA, it is used as a way to tentatively agree on each proposal. It is understood that changes could still be made in the final version, but it is a good faith method to keep track of what has been agreed.

trade-off. The same as *quid pro quo.* In negotiations, it means *I will give you what you want if you give me what I want.* Both parties can get what they want, and the problem is solved.

venting. A way to clear emotions such as anger and frustration so the parties are ready for bargaining. It is a way to let go, like screaming. By expressing emotions, it clears the way for negotiations to take place. Often the first session of a negotiation or mediation will let the parties vent so that the procedure can go to the next step.

vesting. The waiting period for the employee to wait before he qualifies for the employer's retirement benefit. The vesting period can vary from one to ten years.

walkaway. A variation of *take it or leave it.* If you don't give me what I want, then I will quit or walk away.

unfair labor practice. A violation of federal or state labor law.

APPENDIX B
Traits of a Good Negotiator

1. Calm, cool, collected
2. Compassionate
3. Creative
4. Ethical
5. Fair
6. Firm
7. Flexible
8. Good listener
9. Honest
10. nowledgeable
11. Patient
12. Perceptive
13. Persistent
14. Personable
15. Reasonable
16. Respectful
17. Sense of humor
18. Sincere
19. Thinks before speaking
20. Thinks outside the box

APPENDIX C
Sample Ground Rules Policies

A. *Two-Party Ground Rules*

1. Preliminaries: location, table setup, number on team, cell phone rules.
2. Agenda for each meeting.
3. Everyone will speak with courtesy and there will be no profanity.
4. Meetings will start on time and last no more than _____hours.
5. Proposals will be submitted in writing at the _____ meeting.
6. Those sections to be negotiated will be selected by the ___meeting.
7. Either party can call a caucus but will let the other party know if it will last more than twenty minutes.
8. Both parties agree to comply with reasonable requests for information and requesting party will pay reasonable reproduction costs.
9. The parties will confirm the date of next negotiation session at the close of every session.

B. *Negotiating Team Ground Rules*

1. Chief negotiator is chief spokesperson.
2. Chief spokesperson is only person authorized to accept or reject proposals.
3. Everyone speaks through chief spokesperson.
4. Each team member has a role.
5. Nothing is discussed about negotiations except to the team.
6. If a team member wants to speak, he should write a note to call a caucus.
7. Negotiation documents should be kept secure.
8. All team members must attend all negotiation sessions.
9. Nothing should be discussed at a session unless the team has already agreed.

APPENDIX D
About the Author

Mary Greenwood has been an attorney, negotiator, mediator, arbitrator, law school professor, human resources professional, and author of three award-winning books: *How to Negotiate Like a Pro: 41 Rules for Resolving Disputes (1ˢᵗ and 2ⁿᵈ editions); winner of nine book awards, How to Mediate Like a Pro, 42 Rules for Mediating Disputes,* winner of twelve book awards; and *How to Interview Like a Pro: 43 Rules for Getting Your Next Job,* winner of twelve book awards. *How to Negotiate Like a Pro* and *How to Mediate Like a Pro* were both published in India and Kenya. She has also written *Hiring, Firing and Supervising Employees: An Employer's Guide to Discrimination Laws.*

Greenwood has an MA in English from the University of Southern California, a BA in English from the New School University, a JD in law from California Western School of Law, and an LLM in Labor Law from George Washington Law School.

She has worked as head of human resources and union negotiator at Winter Park, Miami Beach, Hollywood, Monroe County, Keys Energy Services (Key West), and Roger Williams University. She has worked as legal counsel at Colorado College, University of North Carolina-Greensboro, Winthrop University, Monroe County, and Manatee County. She has taught labor law, discrimination law, and education law at Stetson Law School, St. Thomas Law School, Barry Law School, Troy State, St. Leo's, and Winthrop University. She was also a book reviewer for the St. Augustine Record.

Greenwood's books have been used as college textbooks in negotiations and mediation courses at the University of Alaska, Nova Southeastern University,

Brown, University of Central Florida, DePaul University and North Texas University

Greenwood has been quoted in the Business News Daily, Money Magazine, the New York Daily News, Real Simple, Kiplinger Retirement Report, The Orlando Sentinel, Media Bistro, State Farm Magazine, CBS Money Watch, Mediation Digest, and Real Simple.

She lives in Florida with her Boston terrier, Annabelle.

Visit www.MaryGreenwood.org.

APPENDIX E
Book Awards

***How to Negotiate Like a Pro,* Winner of nine book awards:**

1. Winner, DIY Book Festival, *How To*
2. Winner, Indie Excellence Book Awards, *Self-help*
3. Finalist, Best National Book Awards, *Self-help*
4. Finalist, ForeWord Magazine Book of the Year Awards, *Self-help*
5. Finalist, Readers Favorite Book Awards, *Self-Help*
6. Finalist, International Book Awards, *Business/Finance*
7. Runner-up, New York Book Festival, *E-Book*
8. Runner-up, New York Book Festival, *Self-help*
9. Honorable Mention, London Book Festival, *Self-help*

***How to Mediate Like a Pro,* Winner of twelve book awards:**

1. Winner, Reader Views, Book Awards, *How To*
2. Winner, Best National Book Awards, *Law*
3. Finalist, Next Generation Indie Books, *Business*
4. Winner, Indie Excellence Awards, *E-Book*
5. Winner, Beach Book Festival, *How To*
6. Winner, New York Book Festival, *E-Book*
7. Winner, Pinnacle Book Achievement Award
8. Silver Prize, ForeWord Book Awards, *Self-help*
9. Runner-up, DIY Book Festival, *E-Book*
10. Spirit Award, South Florida Writers Association
11. Runner-up, New England Book Festival, *How To*
12. Runner-up, London Book Festival, *E-Book*

How to Interview Like a Pro, **Winner of twelve book awards.**

1. Winner, Reader Views Book Awards, *How To*
2. Winner, Pinnacle Book Achievement Awards, *Business*
3. Winner, Indie Excellence Awards, *Career*
4. Winner, Silver Award, ForeWord Book Awards, *Career*
5. Finalist, International Book Awards, *Career*
6. Finalist, Eric Hoffer Book Awards
7. Finalist, Next Generation Indie Book Awards, *Career*
8. Finalist, USA Book News, *Business/Finance*
9. Honorable Mention, Readers Favorites, *Business*
10. Honorable Mention, DIY Book Awards, *How To*
11. Honorable Mention, New York Book Festival, *How To*
12. Extra Mention, Millennium Publishing Book Awards

Printed in the United States
By Bookmasters